HOW ROBOTS IMPROVE PERFORMANCE

JOHN LOK

Contents

Foreword

Introduction

Nowadays, artificial intelligent robotic technology which is one kind of popular tool to help workers to work in factories or offices or serve clients in restaurants or shopping centers. It brings this question: Can artificial intelligent robotic machine men assist workers to raise productive efficiencies or improve service performance? ? All workers are replaced by artificial intelligent robotic machine or some workers are replaced by artificial intelligent robotic machine which can raise more productive efficiencies or improve better service performace ?

If one factory or one office only applies artificial intelligent robotic machine men to replace human labors to help its different departments to do any tasks, whether can its (AI) robotic machine men help them to raise productive efficiencies ? If one restaurant or one shopping center only apply (AI) robotic machine men to help to serve clients, whether can its (AI) robotic machine men help them to improve service performance? Is it better to apply half manual labors and half (AI) robotic machine men to work in one organization in order to raise productive efficiencies or improve service performance?

In my this book, I shall indicate some cases to explain how and why (AI) robotic machine men can either raise productive efficiencies or improve service performance or they can't either raise productive efficiencies or improve service performance in any situations. Managers or employees can evaluate whether how to apply (AI) robotic machine men to assist them to work in their workplaces in order to achieve the most beneficial advantages to their organization's different departments' raising productivity and efficiency and service performance improvement aims.

Prologue

Why and how human behavior may influence the country's economic growth or recession?

Technology how impacts human behavior changing?

How and why employees behaviors may influence economy development?

Robots invention whether they can help organizations to raise efficiencies or inefficiencies?

Why social behavior may influence organizational strategy needs to be changed ?

How and why human behavior may influence economic growth or recession?

CHAPTER ONE

Can Artificial intelligence apply to digital- Transformation on jobs to raise productivity

Future, digital transformative technologies will how impact on economies and societies as well as how (AI) utilization of vast amounts of data to be applied to digital transformative technology. I believe that when (AI) is applied to digital transformative technology which will bring positive impacts on productivity for many firms, but it has not yet translated into stronger productivity growth at the economy –wide level. Larger impacts could result from digital technologies to all firms, notably to small and medium sized enterprises.

However, firms expected that (AI) technology and digital transformative technology can help them to raise productivity , which need have greater investments in critical complementary assets, such as firm-level skills, organizational change and process innovation as well as support for future structural change to enable the growth of new business models and digitally-intensive businesses. However, the (AI) technology is applied to digital transformative technological changes creates significant uncertainty about their future directions and impacts. Indeed, predictions about technological timelines are often inaccurate and over estimate of their short-time impacts is common.

How to achieve (AI) and the internet of things (IOT) and black chain technologies to raise productivities? It depends on large data sets and a range od digital technologies. Strong potential to improve the design implementation and evaluation of organizational policies (strategies of any firms expect to apply (AI) and internet technology combination to raise productivities.

Nowadays, global societies and private organizational firms considerate human centric (AI) needs for societies, and for further information sharing need, deepen the understanding of the potential effects of (AI) technologies on society and economies, ethics, privacy. Job creation issues. Instead of (AI) is constrained to the digital world, with significant activity to influence , such as transport and machinery industry aspects, future (AI) technology can also be applied to service industry, such as healthcare and finance, education and training system in order to raise young people and adults right skills performance and productive efficiencies in an (AI)-enabled environment.

Hence, (AI) transformative and digital technological combination can impact those aspects to influence productivities. On gender influence aspect, Gender is particularly important in ensuring technological transformation of production change working environment. Female and male workers need to learn how to apply (AI) and digital transformative technology to work in offices or factories to strengthen their position in the labor market and in driving the digital transformation in order to achieve the aim of raising productivities. On skills safeguard against the risk of automation influence aspect, fewer than 5% of worker with a tertiary degree are at a high risk of losing their job, due to automation compared to 40% of workers with a lower secondary degree.

In future (AI) and digital technological working environment , workers needed to be equipped with a wide set of skills to be equipped with a wide set of skills as well as non-cognitive and social skills (notably information and communication technology (ICT) skills, science, technology, engineering ad mathematics (STEM) skills, and self-organization skills). Future, (AI) and digital technologies can potentially also promote social inclusion by creating education, offer-new opportunities for skills development, enhance access to healthcare industry or improve access to free and low-cost information, knowledge, and data to help organizations to improve service performance or raise productivity.

How (AI) and digital technological working environment influence job changed for employees. When, it is uncertainty about the speed of changes, it is clear that the types of jobs that are being created are not the same as those that are being lost. Moreover, the workers are affected by job loss in declining activities may not be those benefitting from the new job opportunities in any organizations. The middle –skilled jobs declining and low and high skilled jobs growing. Low –skilled workers are mostly likely to bear the costs of digital transformation, but are currently the least likely to receive training. So, the employers need to apply (AI) and digital technology to raise productivities which will influence some low-skilled workers will lose jobs, unless they can learn how to apply this new (AI) and digital technology to assist them to work in any working environments.

Better understanding the likely scope of the digital transformation and (AI) technology combination is needed to any organizations including: the growth of the big economy, or the impacts on productivity , the growing role of data, including in traditional trade is a particularly important area where sound data , i.e. data on data flow that is lacking . Although, there are still large difference in digital intensity, every firm in every sector in the economy is now being affected by the digital transformation, expanding its scope and its potential benefits. All organizations need to learn how to apply digital technology to assist whose workers to work efficiently in factories or offices in beginning. When they can learn how to apply digital technology to work. Then, they can learn how to apply

(AI) technology and digital technology together to work together in order to achieve raising productivities or improve performance aims. For example, data combined with (AI) and digital technological innovation is online activity and networked things generate " big data" which feed machine learning that enables (AI), to lead to advances in intelligent machines (robotics, automated vehicles) as well as new techniques in science which can be further innovation. The growth of the volume, variety data and the ability to analyze and use it is a significant departure from the past and it causes new factor of production that argues traditional capital and labor, but unique properties of its own to be applied to office or factory manufacturing work environment in order to achieve the raising of productivity or improve performance in possible.

Why does (AI) and digital transformative combination technologies raise productivity growth or improve service performance? From 1995 to 2004 year, US experienced an acceleration in productivity growth, largely reflecting gains associated with the diffusion of ICT technologies. From the early to mid-2000 year onward, productivity growth has slowed down. The potential impacts of the ongoing digital transformation on productivity also need to consider in the context of this long term slowdown. When, the precise reasons for today's productivity remain difficult to a number of factors are likely to contribute as below factors:

The first factor that has limited the impacts of digital transformation is the state of diffusion of digital technologies across the economy. When, many firms now have across to broadband networks, the use of more advanced digital tools and application with firms still differs greatly across countries. Moreover, these are important differences between rapid technological change, advanced technologies are initially only adopted by some leading firms and then only later diffuse to all firms as the technologies because more established new business models grow, such as applying digital and (AI) technological combine method to raise productivity growth is caused and costs fall.

Consequently, these is large demand between what can be automated from a technical point of view and what may already be implemented by frontier firms and what is actually being achieve to raise productivity growth aim. So, (AI) and digital transformative technology influence future raising productivity growth or improving service aim achievement for many manufacturing and service industry demand.

The second factor indicator that the available evidence suggests that the wide-spread benefits of digitalization productivity are not enough. Firms expect to help strengthen investment (in tangible and intangible assets), e.g. (AI) technology. The same time, there are now starting to experience labor shortages, e.g. in certain technical occupations, such as data scientists. Due to the technological change is fast and growing demand for productivity growth has been increasing. SO, it will influence future (AI) robotic learning system and digital technological combination to be applied to manufacturing and service industries' needs to be raised. Due to many firms expect to find methods to raise productivity growth in order to reduce production costs.

However, (AI) and digital technological development can cause multiple forms of disruption, from shifts in demand for workforce skills to changes in market structure, the need for new business models, new patterns of trade and investment. The (AI) and digital potentially transformative technologies can create new inventions, e.g. from quantum computing and advanced energy storage to new forms of 3D printing, big data analytics and neuro-technologies. These new product creative industries must lead the new product manufacturers to expect to learn how to apply (AI) and digital technology to raise productivity growth when their manufacturing processes.

IN fact, (AI) is the ability of learning machine and system to acquire and apply knowledge and carry out intelligent behavior. Early efforts to develop (AI) centered on defining rules that software could use to perform a tack, such systems would work in speech recognition, (AI) skill. Increase in computational power, new statistical methods and advances in big data, have brought major breakthroughs to the field of (AI), especially in " vertical " (AI) like automated vehicles as opposed to " general". (AI) with machine learning algorithms that identify complex patterns in large data sets. Software applications can perform tasks and simultaneously learn how to improve productive performance. Hence, (AI) can be combined to digital world to work together with advanced in electrical engineering, it has robots to perform cognitive task in the physical world. (AI) will enable robots to adapt to new working environments with no reprogramming. Also, (AI) enabled robots will become increasingly central to logistics and manufacturing, complementing and sometimes displacing human labor in many production processes.

Future (AI) will also be developed to apply to service industry, e.g. healthcare, entertainment, marketing and finance industries. Even, future (AI) that recognizes human facial expressions and emotions could help to deliver some public services and possibly educational services. Future an essential factor achieve benefits of (AI) is the provision of reliable energy and communication networks, including for the IOT. Therefore, laws and legal frameworks may need to be considered before many of the benefits of (AI) can be bad in fields, such as transportation and healthcare industries. All above of these industries will need (AI) technology and digital technologies combination to help future manufacturing or service industries both to raise their productivity growth or improve service performance in order to reduce cost or provide more service satisfactory feeling to clients in their manufacturing processes or service processes in any manufacturing or service environments.

1.1 Apply (AI) technology to raise U.S. steel, aluminum, cooper mineral productivity growth

Future (AI) technologic robotic machines can learn how to apply 3D printer to manufacture any size and material of copied steel, aluminum , copper mineral products to be better quality in efficient productivity speed and growth. Global production of aluminum and cooper and steel mineral materials trends for global manufacturing industry is continue increasing needs to use steel, cooper, aluminum minerals to manufacture any products, e.g. car, boats, ships, furnitures, machines, buildings etc. products. However, global any products for above these mineral materials manufacturers will select the most reasonable price and the best quality of any one these minerls to select to manufacture any products which need these mineral materials or component to produce. Hence, global mineral material (component) suppliers will trend to raise these any one of minerals to produce high quality products, long term durable, reasonable price sale demand to sell to consumers.

I shall give opinions to explain that how U.S. steel, aluminum, copper mineral component suppliers need to implement what kinds of sale strategy in order to attract global steel, aluminum, copper, mineral component consumers to select to buy their steel, aluminum, cooper moneral components more easily.

Firstly, I shall discuss iron or steel sector, since the iron and steel contributes considerably to industrial CO_2 emission, it is important to identify the factors driving steel demand. Two major factors will determine future CO_2 emissions in the steel sector. The first is technological progress which could lead to more efficient production technologies. However, coal which is the main source of CO_2 emissions do not only serve as a fuel in the melting process and for casting and rolling the steel. Furthermore needed for the reduction of iron ore, which makes it difficult to trim down its use beyond a certain level, even if substantial progress has been made in corrective direction. So, advanced economies, such as developed country, U.S. any steel manufacturers can attempt to use coke to manufacturer steel more efficiently. Thus, technological process in steel making is one important factor which will drive the steel manufacture and sale industry's future CO_2 emissions. The other majoe factor driving CO_2 emissions from the steel sector is future global steel demand.

In past history , in the mid-1960 year, the industry reconstruction period, which led to an increase in steel demand and production. In this period, the advanced economies were the main drivers of global steel demand. So, new production techniques are needs to global steel manufacturers. Then 1990 year, the global steel demand began to grow when many products which need steel mineral component to manufacture. In fact, steel consumption demand growth depends on two factors as below:

The first considers the industry sector and its structure , it means whether how many products need steel mineral to be supplied to manufacturer. The second considers the country's income of its population and its demand for steel manufacturing products. Hence, any U.S. steel manufacturers need to consider what kinds of unique industries which are developing in the country in order to predict the country's steel demand more accurately. For example, China's car manufacturing industry needs many steel to manufacture cars. Hence, U.S. steel manufactuers can research what steel quality, shape, price are the most attraction to sell to China car manufacturers. So, as above explanation, high technological steel manufacturing method will be one important factor to influence future U.S. steel manufacturing industry export market in success. Due to other countries which have some steel sells and some steel manufacturers who can have high technology to manufacture steel , e.g. Germany is one successful steel manufacturing country because its steel manufacturing skill had reached mature stage. Hence, U.S. needs have advanced steel manufacturing technology to raise its stel quality to win its competitors.

Hence, nowadays, global steel manufacturing industry is increasing competition. Due to the relationship between steel use and per-capita income is close. Steel consumers (steel using product manufacturers) consider to measure of technological process how the steel manufactuers apply high technology to manufacture steel products. So, high technological steel manufacturing method will be one important factor to influence steel consumers (steel using product manufacturers, e.g. car manufacturer) to select to buy their steel products in nowadays global steel manufacturing industry. Hence, U.S. steel manufacturing factories need high technological equipment to help them to manufacture the best quality, the most long durable time steel products in order to attract global steel useful steel product manufacturers to select to buy U.S.'s steel products more easily.

On income hand, it concerns global steel useful product manufacturers' income (profit), it means that U.S. steel manufacturers need to know and evaluate whether how much profit past and future global steel useful manufacturer's product consumers (business clients) that they will earn or they had earned in order to predict whether how much steel number which they will buy. It is important reason to explain why U.S. steel manufacturers need to know how much profit their business clients will earn because tehe U.S. steel manufacturers can predict whom will be their next year clients. For example, if the country one steel mineral (component) useful product manufacturing client who had loss last year. it is possible that who will reduce to buy the U.S. steel manufacturer's steel product number to prepare to manufacture how much steel number is the most accurate because its client number is less to cause loss, even it won't need any steel need to prepare to manufacture more products, e.g. cars to raise sale. Otherwise, if the country one steel mineral (component) useful product manufacturing client who had profit last year, it is possible that who will increase to buy steel products number to prepare to raise many steel mineral manufacturing need of products, e.g. cars in order to satisfy many car clients' needs in possible. So, it is possible that they (the car manufactuers) need to buy much steel to prepare to manufacture their products in this year.

Conclusion, U.S. steel manufacturers need to evaluate global steel consumers or business clients whose past and present and future financial performance in order to predict how much steel number they will need to buy as well as they also need to raise steel manufacturing equipment efficiency and performance and quality in order to raise steel productivities and qualities to keep its long time durable useful value to satisfy every steel manufacturing products' consumer' needs, e.g. cars. Hence, these two factors will be future U.S. steel manufacturing suppliers who need to concern issue in order to attract global steel mineral (component) buyers' competitive good quality of steel products needs to achieve preferable selection to their U.S. steel products to buy in global steel competitive market.

Secondly, I shall indicate U.S. aluminum, cooper, mineral manufacturing industry is similar to steel mineral manufacturing industry, but they have different competitive sale strategy. I shall explain as below:

In the future, it will be how trends in consumption and global production to select minerals of aluminium and cooper. Nowadays, to growth rate of primary production of aluminum and cooper. So, it causes threat to aluminum and cooper need for industry use, due to recycling technology can bring recycle re-use of aluminum and cooper nature to help industries to re-use any aluminum and cooper resources element to manufacture any products. So, the future trend of aluminum and cooper resources element will be reduced to global industries needs because recycling technology can bring cost benefits to let them to use recycling aluminum and cooper element. So, new aluminum and cooper resource element needs will be reduced.

Otherwise, the recycling re-used aluminum and cooper resources element has been re-used many times for the product manufacturers. Amyway, the manufacturers won't easier to select to buy new aluminum and cooper resource element. Although, the production of both primary and second recycled aluminum both have increased in fact speed. For most countries, there are no data to distinguish between production of secondary aluminum from past-consumer scrap (discarded aluminum products) and new (manufacturing) scrap. But, it seems, future trend of recycling secondary aluminum product demand is more than primary new aluminum product demand in global manufacturing industry market, such data indicated U.S. hich accounts for 50% of total world secondary aluminum product. So, it seems that secondary aluminum product (recycled) will be demanded more than primary new aluminum production. It also indicated U.S. 59% of the secondary aluminum was recovered from new scrap and 41% from post-consumer scrape. Hence, if implies future aluminum manufacturing industry consumers will select to buy secondary aluminum (recycling products) more than primary new aluminum non-used products. So, future trend in aluminum recycling product need will be reduced when nowadays aluminum resource element had been recycled to manufacture again new recycling elements many times to supply to global steel product manufacturers to re-use these nowadays recycling aluminum resource elements many times again.

I believe that future one day, when these nowadays secondary recycling aluminum resources elements had been used many times by global any product manufacturers. Then, they can be recycled to manufacture these old recycling aluminum resource element again. The effect will be that they can not be recycled to manufacture again because they had been recycled to manufactured many times. Their quality will be worst to compare primary (new) aluminum resource element to let global product manufacturers to use them to manufacture high quality of products to sell. So, I predict future primary new aluminum or cooper need will be increased because the second recycling aluminum or cooper resource element had been recycled to used to manufacture new products by different manufacturers many times. So, future the primary (new) aluminum or coooper need will be increased an dprice can also be influenced to be raised. Thus, I recommend that U.S. aluminum or cooper industrial manufacturing resource element manufacturers ought need to prepare how to seek new natural resource to manufacture primary (new) aluminum or cooper products and they ought not only concentrate on gathering reused aluminum or cooper to manufacture them again. Because , future global aluminum or cooper product consumers will prefer select to buy primary (new) aluminum or cooper more thn secondary recycling aluminum or cooper to help them to do any products to sell. So, future new (primary) aluminum or cooper product will be more proper to compare secondary recycling aluminum or cooper to seel in global industrial manufacturing market.

CHAPTER TWO

Can robots raise productive efficiency to raise logistic transportation speed

Can (AI) raise productive efficiency to logistic industrial sector? Technological progress in the fields of big data, algorithmic development, connectivity , cloud computing have made the performances, accessibility and costs of (AI) more favorable. Logistics is beginning to become an (AI)- driven industry, but it has also encountered challenges to overcome and opportunities to exploit. As in other industries, (AI) will extend human efficiency in terms of reach quality and speed by eliminating routine work. This will allow logistic workforces to focus in more meaningful and impactful work.

How can (AI) raise productive growth efficiency or fast manufacturing speed to logistic industry? (AI) can be defined as human intelligence exhibited by machines, syustems that approximate, replicate, automate and eventually improve on human thinking . It owns the ability to perceive , understand, learn , problem solve and reason. Whereas, (AI) is a system or device intended to amount with intelligence, machine learning is a more specific to taken in formation, usually within a specific domain, and learn from what they have been given. These learning systems draw on the ability to evaluate and categorize received data and then draw inferences from this. The output of this process is an insight decision or conclusion.

(AI) technology consists of sensing, components, processing components and learning components. SO, (IA) has this analytical process: (AI) can have deep learning ability to improve to process and understand unstructured data, e.gf. text, image, sound , then data gathered continuously from the environment, sensors and online behavior and data is aggregated. Next, machine learning framework begins to process data, patterns and trends are revealed, generated insight. Finally, the (AI) learning system takes different actions to drive value. New action is used as input to improve self-learning of system. IT is any (AI)'s full learning cycle in (AI) analytical process.

How can (AI) apply its supervised learning skills to raise productive efficiency to logistic industry? The processing and learning components and training techniques to (AI) includes" Once an (AI) system has collected data from sensing, it processes this information by applying a learning framework to generate insight from the data. IN addition to the similarities that exist between human intelligence and (AI) , strong parallels have also been observed between how humans and (AI) learning systems.

In the future, (AI) can be such a supervised learning machine man to supervise logistic workers and control and manage them how to deliver goods in warehouses more efficient. Even, they can replace human logistic workers to do their logistic tasks in warehouses. What is (AI) supervised learning system mean : It is learning that takes place when an (AI) –enabled system is directly informed by humans. I shall explain it as doctor case, A doctor who evaluates x-ray images to detect cancer risk, he/she can feed whose expert input images into an (AI) learning system to facilities supervised learning or when the (AI) learning system sorts through x-ray images for a doctor to review and approve in an effort to help improve the learning of the (AI) learning system. So, it seems that

(AI) learning system can be applied to do any supervising tasks. When, (AI) robotic machines are applied to logistic warehouse environment, it can be one artificial intelligent supervisor to check any products whether are delivered to the exact locations or shelfs as well as the number of products whether it is accurate to be prepared to delivery to the outsider accurate destinations before all goods are already sent out from the warehouses. For example, Amazon publish company paper book buyers need to buy paper books , when they pay visa payment and every reader choose the right topic book from its website, when they choose to buy the topic of paper book, then Amazon publish will send the reader 's the topic book choice to its warehouse. When the logistic worker know what the topic of the paper book is sold, then the (AI) learning system will record the topic of the book and the country address of the paper book buyer to already to print the topic of paper book and send to the book buyer's address. Due to , there are many different countries paper book buyers who had chosen the different topic books to buy from amazon publish website. For example, if there are five hundred different countries book buyers who had paid visa to buy different topic books from Amazon publish website in the same day. Then , Amazon publish needs to deliver these five hundred different countries paper book buyers overseas address and the warehouse workers need to print all these five hundred different topic paper books in the same time in order to deliver all these five hundred paper books to their overseas home within two days. If Amazon publish has none of (AI) learning system to help it to record this five hundred different topic paper book buyers' overseas correct addresses and the accurate topic of every book. Then , I believe that Amazon publish has no more confidence to print the accurate different paper book right topic number and record all the different countries paper book buyers' overseas home addresses and names in order to print and deliver to them from warehouse within two days. SO, (AI) learning system can help this electronic publishing firm to record all these five hundred different countries paper book buyers' addresses and every paper book topic in its centered logistic system efficiently and effectively. Amazon publish can reduce some warehouse workers number , due to it has (AI) learning system to help it to record all paper book buyer's address and name and book topic clearly. Even, (AI) robotic machine men can help it to deliver any book to the accurate shelf location in order to delivery the right topic of every book to post to the right country's book buyer's address before all these five hundred different topic books are already posted to their overseas addresses by air planes. SO, (AI) learning system and robotics can help this publisher to manage and supervise all warehouse workers how to put these five hundred paper books to the different shelves locations more accurate in this day in warehouse. If it lacks(AI) learning system and robotic warehouse machine man to assist its warehouse workers to work in warehouse. It will increase the risk to post the wrong topic book to the wrong book buyer's address.

However, in logistic industry (AI) learning system applying key challenge facing the progress of (AI) is that logistic industry users do not trust it, because they still feel (AI) learning system can't supervise workers to deliver and distribute any products to achieve 100% accuracy in warehouses confidently. So I recommend that , the returns on (AI) investments are already improving in logistic industry and the growth in customer –facing commercial areas clearly indicates the use of (AI) learning systems and robotics in industrial sectors, such as logistic is quickly approaching. Furthermore, future many logistic companies depend on networks both physical and increasingly digital, which must function to bring these benefits, such as high products volumes and accurate numbers delivery, learn asset allocation, low margins and time-sensitive deadlines. SO, (AI) learning system and robotic machine men can offer logistic companies the ability to optimize network to degrees of efficiency and accurate number of different kinds of product deliveries, such as Amazon publish warehouse different topic printed books are delivered to overseas readers case. (AI) can also help the logistic industry to definite warehouse delivery behaviors and practices, taking operations from reactive to proactive , planning from forecast to prediction ,process from manual to autonomous, and services from standardized to personalized, warehouse delivery needs . For IBM computer products warehouse delivery case example, (AI) learning system can apply network to help IBM computer manufacturing workers to grow productivity and effectiveness of individual knowledge workers. They can be IBM manufacturing workers' assistants to assist them to manufacture any kinds of computer products in warehouse more efficiently. It can bring reducing time spending to manufacturers and (AI) robotic machine manufacturers both manufacture every computers' parts or components together in IBM warehouses. It will bring the benefits include: reducing manufacturing spending time, high productivity growth, high efficiency, avoiding manufacturing errors occurrence in IBM computer every manufacturing process.

The use of (AI) engineering and manufacturing signals a departure from the purely digital world. It can now shape the physical world around us. The manufacturing conglomerate general electric is ways to deliver power, energy and air travel. Part of the answer may be to use (AI) to inform, the production requirements and manage the continuous operation of heavy machinery to supervise products distribution, supply chain into one intelligent system in logistic warehouses. The system is connected to an intelligent order management system. Once the problem is understood and the required parts are identifies from the images , the correct parts order can be placed automatically . Finally, if specialist intervention is needed, the smart manufacturing platform can check the technician's schedule and suggest the best times for maintenance in warehouses. So, A(I) learning system can be also applied to supervise and manage warehouse works in warehouses.

Why can (AI) learning system raise productivity growth in logistic industry warehouses? (AI) learning system can be value add chain by automating existing business processes, uncovering new chain add value from data and augmenting logistic management decisions and actions . The ability to analyze levels of data that are beyond human comprehension allows logistic businesses to personalize, fast speed logistic experiences, customize products and logistic deliver services and identify productivity growth opportunities with a speed and precision that has never been positive before.

Hence, future (AI) learning system may be applied to those logistic industries , such as below:

On accurate demand forecasting beneficial aspect, in retail industry improved 1 to 2 % logistic speed to transport , improvement using machine learning to anticipate fruit and vegetable sales, 20% stock reduction using deep learning to predict e-commerce purchases, fewer product returns per year; in electric utilities industry, it can achieve objective to cut 10% in natural electricity usage by using deep learning to predict power demand and supply; on higher productivity and maintenance and repairs aspect, in retail industry , (AI) learning system has 30% reduction of stocking time using autonomous vehicles in warehouses; in electric utilities industry, (AI) learning system has 20% energy production increase using machine learning and smart sensors to optimize assets' yield as well as 10 to 20% improvement by using machine learning to enhance predictive maintenance , automate fault prediction and increase capital productivity; in manufacturing industry, (AI) learning system has 30% increase of machines delivery time using machine learning to determine timing of products' transfer and 3 to 5% production yield can be improved.

In conclusion, future (AI) learning system can enable massive productivity gains for logistic industry automating their process. Logistic industry can combine with the industrial internet of things, achieve learning can predict anomalies and sensor data, image videos and audio data and therefore reduce losses in warehouses. Moreover, manufacturers for instance are using machine learning and other (AI) techniques to better predict failure and thus to reduce maintenance costs in warehouses.

2.1 Apply (AI) technology to improve fruit and vegetable soft drink logistic transportation speed in efficient way in warehouse

Future (AI) robotic machines can be applied to help logistic workers to deliver the accurate number and weight and the right different kinds of fruit and vegetable to different locations in efficient way in warehouses. State of the plate (2015) indicated that the U.S. fruit and vegetable consumption market trend after a brief rise through 2005 year, US per capita fruit and vegatable consumption has declined 7% over the past five years, this has been driven primarily by decreased consumption of vegetables (-7%) and fruit juice (-14%). If fruit juice is excluded from the overall furit total. However, these is only a 2% decrease in fruit consumption over the past 5 year. So, fruit has seen growth among certain subsets of the population, specifically children of all ages and adult ages 18 to 44 age.

Hence, it seems that fruit juice is popular to be selected to drink for chikdren and young, adult consumers in U.S. food market. Otherwise, U.S. consumers can select either to buy fresh fruit and vegetable to eat or buy fruit juice and vegetable juice to drink in U.S. fruit and vegetable health food market. However, U.S. food consumers will have possible to decrease fruit and/or vegetable soft drink consumption. The factors include ongoing interest in consuming loe-carbohydrate foods, which peaked a decade ago, and the ever-increasing competitive set of beverages available to consumers that include flavored water. So, U.S. fruit or vegetable soft drink consumers will have possible to reduce fruit or vegetable soft drink consumption because they feel flavored water beverges or fresh fruit and vegetable will be low-carbohydrate food. Otherwise, fruit and vegetables soft drink are " sugar-sweetened" beverages. It will give less health to compare fresh fruit or vegetable food.

Why is fruit or vegetable food the main food to U.S. people daily? The reasons include that : In U.S. eating habit, fruit has enjoyed gains in U.S. people traditional consumption habit t breakfast. This is likely because breakfast is a more health related meal and fruit. For example, berries and bananas have gained favor all day, probably due to their versatility for consumption and these both fruits are as a topping for cereal or yogurt or as an ingiedient to a smoothie or hot cereal.

Future global children and young and adult and old age food consumers whether they will change their eating habit to accept fruit and vegetable soft drink to replace fresh druit and vegetable food more easily. I believe that every different age fruit and vegetable food consumer targets who will have different food need. For old age fruit and vegetable food consumer target , U.S. fruit and vegetable soft drink manufacturers need to persuade old age fruit and vegetable consumers to change their fresh fruit and vegetable food eating habit for better medical conditions , it is as a category to bring stronger health benefit to persuade higher consumption rates among older consumers. Global many old age people are concerning their health and greater incidence of medical conditions.

In specially, for the consumer ages 50 or above. Their eating habits are usually to select fresh fruit and vegetable to eat. So , it is more difficult to change their eating habits to select fruit and vegetable soft drink more easily. Unless, U.S. fruit and vegetable soft drink manufacturers can find some strong points which can influence global old people feel fruit and vegetable are not meeting in terms of their health and daily lives. Other influential factors which will be possible to influence their food and fruithabit changing to select fruit and vegetable for their daily lives need, e.g. reasonable price, better taste, shopping convenience. For example, yogurt is a natural gaining for fruit or vegetable and some fruit can work well on pizza or a variety of vegetables can be included on poultry sandwiches. All of these complementary food groups are also among th fastest growing food items. They can have much competitive effort to influence global traditional fresh fruit and vegetable consumers to select to buy these kinds of complementary fruit and vegetable to eat sometimes in daily lives because they can provide fresh taste of food choice, due to their taste will have some different feeling to let global fresh fruit and vegetable consumers to fee when they are eating. Also, choice of anywhere locations to sell fruit and/or vegetable soft drink, this factor is also important. In retail, these has been a lot of focus on the perimeter of the store, but the center of the fruit and vegetable soft drink store location is important and fruit and vegetable soft drink or yougurt natural drink for fruit product or vegetables and some fruit pizza or a variety of vegetables include on sandwiches which can be sold on different countries' cities restaurants or food retail shops or pizza retail stores which can be selected to locate to any country's central cities in order to attract travellers or working people to find these restaurants conveniently to buy different kinds of manual manufacturing of fruit and/or vegetable taste of soft drink or food restaurants to drink or eat for breakfast, lunch or dinner.

In conclusion, the future global future fruit and vegetable soft drink consumption influential factors will include taste, retail locaion choice, drink or food element manufacturing factor in order to attract global fresh fruit or fresh vegetable food consumers' consideration If U.S. fruit and vegetable soft drink food manufacturers expect to change global fruit and vegetable food consumers' traditional eating habits easily. They must have good sale plans for how to maufacture attractive taste, how to select suitable locations to sell and how to charge the price to let global different fruit and vegetable food consumers to feel their fruit and vegetable soft drink products are more reasonable price to compare traditional fresh fruit and vegetable food. However, fruit and vegetable will have possible to be not fresh when they are saved long time in any stores or farms location. Otherwise, fruit and vegetable soft drink will have long time to save to ice box to wait to drink. So, it is maunal manufacturing of fruit and vegetable soft drink food product's stronger point to compete to natural fruit and vegetable food.

2.2 Applying (AI) technology to improve global daily food logistic transporation speed in warehouses

Future (AI) robotic machines can assist warehouse workers to deliver the accurate number and right different kinds of daily drinks, e.g. milk, orange juice, apply juice, soft drinks, milk, cheese, ice-cream etc. different kinds of soft drinks and food to different right loacations in efficient way and the fast transportation speed in warehouses. The research and insights committee indicated that it discovered U.S. daily food industry had no loger significant increases in gross dometic product and population expansion to drive domestic growth. So, it brings this challenge for U.S. daily food product manufacturers' cost savings / gains driven and production efficiencies will be possible caused to U.S. daily food product caused to U.S. daily food product manufacturers in domestic market. So, they ought consider how to expand overseas daily food product market to attempt to increase more different kinds of daily products to different countries. I shall recommend some solutions as below:

U.S. daily food product manufacturers ought plan future five to ten year opportunities to drive the growth of daily / daily -based food products to overseas different countried. For example, Hong Kong, China, Japan Asia countries have many people who like to buy U.S. daily food to eat or drink, e.g. milk, cheese, ice-cream. So, they need have good identification of macro trends and a greater understanding of data-based key elements (e.g. the country's demographic shifts, prediction of the country has how many people who like to eat or drink any kinds of daily food, e.g. Japan's one city Tokyo has how many people who like to eat or drink any kinds of U.S. daily food ; finding every country's people whose food / eating behaviors, e.g. in what suitation which will influence Japanese have desire to buy daily food, such as the consumption group , e.g. prediction of young or old age Japanese number will like to eat or drink U.S. daily food in what time of one day for the old or young age Japaneses' eating habit, e.g. morning time, luch time or dinner time. So, the U.S. daily food manufactuers can follow the suitable time to prepare sell the accurate number to Japan. For example, if they predict there are 500,000 about Japanese young and old age people who like to buy U.S. daily food to eat or drink after dinner time in Tokyo city every week. Then, they can export enough different kinds of daily food number to Tokyo every week ; retail channel shift , e.g. supermarket ot small retil store ; food service promotion perspective , .e.g. newspaper or magazone or radio daily food service promotion channel choice to let the country people to know what kinds of U.S. daily food can be sole to the country. Then, these methods can help any U.S. daily food manufacturers have potential to predict the accurate consumption number to every coutries and U.S. itself to raise their daily food export or local sale number.

These methods aim to investigate whether what kinds of daily food products sale to the country's people who will be accepted to buy to eat or drink more. For example, how many Japanese are living in the city , e.g. Tokyo , who like to buy milk, daily beverages, cheeses, yogurt, frozen daily and daily is as an ingredient or a component food to eat or drink. Thus, market research can help the U.S. daily food manufacturers to attempt to predict every export country's different cities daily food product buyer number and predict what kinds of daily food will be popular to choose to eat or drink for the country's different cities' peoples' eating culture or habit. So, U.S. daily food manufacturers need have a leading global strategic planning to predict future how consumer insights and trends will how and why and when change in order to make more accurate daily food customer behavioral predictive analysis to satisfy the country's daily food product consumer need and making the more accurate suitable population daily food sale distribution for different kinds of daily food products to the country.

The daily food market research strategiss plan will be marked by increasing rates of change driven by key macro forces as below:

Firstly, U.S. daily food manufacturers need to evaluate uncertainty over policies, economy, supply and different kinds of daily food prices will be possible to increase traditional middle income Americans and global daily food consumer number. It depends on their brands whether are familiar to their daily food consumers because U.S. daily food industry will need to evaluate how global market environment economic changes and daily food product supply is predicted to the different kinds of sale number and global daily food product consumer's demand in order to measure the most accurate sale price to different kinds of daily food to let global daily food consumers to feel the brand of daily food suppliers' sale prices are more reasonable in order to raise its consumer number and define the both low-end (social reasonable acceptance of premium sale price strategy) in global competitive daily food market.

Secondly, U.S, daily food manufacturers need to innovate or improve their manufacturing method to raise different kinds of daily food products' qualities, improving daily food product formulation , e.g. taste, health food elements, attractive daily food and consumer beneficial package and advertising doctors' medical health confirmation message offerings to let global daily food consumers to know. Due to nowadays, global (including U.S.) daily food product consumer number will be increasingly diverse and more globally aware (aging population, growing and extending to a more diverse youth demographic daily food product consumer trend). The changing face and resultant health conditions of global daily food product consumers will require daily food as well as brands of different kinds of daily health food products' food health quality will be needed to raise in order to satisfy their health food needs.

Finally, smart shopping technology will be increasing demand to U.S. different brands of daily food manufacturers. Global health daily food consumers will choose to buy any kinds of daily food from digital technology, i.e. online shopping is one kind of fast long distance distance point of purchase decision making capabilities. Also, smart shopping technology will alter and raise global daily food product consumers' health food expectations of retail to more of an experience. So, how to select sale channels to buy the brand's daily health food which will be one important factor to influence every brand of daily food product manufacturer in success because global daily food product consumers had been influenced by internet onlye shopping channel. For example, U.S. some daily food consumer who are living far away from cities, if their home locations has no any supermarkets, and they need to drive long time to arrive the locations where have supermarkets. Then, they need to choose to buy any kinds of daily food products from internet because daily food product price is cheap and purchase number is less. So, they will compare the journey of their gas spending needed to drive their cars and driving time from homes to supermarkets as well as internet online shopping channel.

Usually, if U.S. daily food product consumers will prefer to choose to buy these kinds of daily food from internet channel when they need to drive cars to go o supermarkets. The reasons is because that they can earn more economic benefits of less time and less cost from internet online shopping channel to compare driving cars to go to supermarkets channel to buy the only daily food product every time. For example, their daily food today sale product include, yogurt, cheese, fozen food etc. these kinds of daily food products which are the most popular to buy from internet online channel for the living far away supermarkets to satisfy lower order convenience needs for internet online shopping channel. This reason is supported on behavioral economic theory to explain why internet online shopping channel is more acceptance to the living far away from supermarkets.

In conclusion, any brands of U.S. daily food product manufacturers ought consider these above any strategies in order to raise their competitive effort in global daily food product market in success more easily. When they apply (AI) learning system technology to improve their transportation speed efficiently.

2.3 Applying (AI) technology improve U.S. future alcohol, wine drink products logistic transportation speed in warehouses

Future (AI) robotic mahcines can assist warehouse workers to transport the accurate number of right alcohol, wine drink products to different locations in efficient speed in warehouses.Nowadays, some economists predicted U.S. to be the largest wine, alcohol the largest drinking consumer. What are the factors cause U.S. has effort to be grown demand in global wine or alcohol industry. I shall follow the global economic changing factors to estimate how and why global wine consumers' behaviors are influenced to choose to buy U.S. wine or alcohol by global economic changing factor influences.

One reason is found evidence which is based on winr or alcohol quantify determinants of global wine consumption influence. It seems that U.S. every year wine or alcohol manufacturing number will influence global wine or global consumers why to choose U.S. wine or alcohol to drink. I shall explain why economic factor will influence U.S. wine supply number. For example, when the year, it has oversupply of grapes to import to U.S. for wine manufacturers to manufacture and kinds of wine drinking products, which made possible the introduction of extreme value wines in U.S. country.

When the global economic environment is good, many people has jobs to work. Then, it will cause many people consider to choose to buy the better quality of different kinds of wine to drink, due to global many people have extra money to save. They have effort to spend to drink at lest one bottle better quality of wine to drink. Thus, the global wine drinker number will increse. With the rise in per capita income in U.S. itself country and other countries as well as the year oversupply of grapes import number can be supplies to let U.S. any wine manufacturers to manufacture different kinds of better quality wine in order to sell to overseas and U.S. domestic wine drinkers. Thus, in the year, the demand for higher qiality food and beverages , e.g. wine is expected to rise , due to the year economic environment is good and U.S. oversupply number of grape to prepare to manufacture different kinds of better quality wine in order to satisfy global high quality wine drinkers' taste needs.

Hence, it proves that global economic environment changing factor and U.S. better quality of wine supply factor will influence U.S. wine drinker number. If the year economic environment is bad, global many people lose jobs and the farming growth environment is poor, it has not good climate to grow many grapes to rise their number for U.S. wine manufacturers to manufacture any kinds of wine products. Then, U.S. wine supply number and global better quality of wine drinker number both will decrease. Thus, global economic environment and U.S. better quality of wine drinkers' demand will have direct or indirect relationship to influence U.S. wine sale number.

Other U.S. wine export number successful factor considers U.S. wine manufacturers ought consider different countries' wine drinkers' taste , reasonable sale price demand and their drinking wine culture (drinking habit). Historically, U.S. wineries adopter either of three methods to sell any kinds of wines drinking product. They include lifestyle, product or production. I shall explain as below;

Firstly, lifestyle means tht every country's wine consumers will have themselves wine drinking culture or habit to choose which kinds of wine or alcohol drinking product to drink. So, if any U.S. wine drink product manufacturers can know the country's wine consumers' preferable wine product choice.

Then, they can evaluate whether which kinds of wine product to decide to sell to the country more accurate and easily, product of wine. It means that they can know how to produce high quality wine products, e.g. using how much grapes or lemons or oranges or apples etc. fruit element and sugar and how to keep the suitable temperature to save every bottle of wine in wine stores in whole wine manufacturing procedure efficiently in order to manufacture the best taste of different kinds of fruit wine to sell to the different countries' target consumers to sell. Because different countries' wine consumers who have different taste preferable needs and wine qualities and drinking culture (habit) needs. So, they need to gather data concerns different countries' wine drinking consumers' preferable choice needs in order to choose the best suitable kinds of wine taste to sell to the country prope to drink.

Finally, it is production cost aspect, it concerns how much costs of every kind wine to manufacture every kind of wine products. It is very important to influence every U.S. wine suppliers' consumer number because if it's production cost, e.g. finished wine product lorry transportation cost in U.S. domestic places between the wine manufactuer's factory and wine stores or fruit transportation farming places and its wine manufacturer's factory which transportat cost is high as well as overseas air plane fruit transportation cost to be delivered the wine manufacturer's factory or the U.S. finished wine products are needed to transport to overseas wine market to sell to different countries' air plane freight cost which is high, then these transportation cost will influence the U.S. wine seller's sale price to be raised if it needs often to deliver any wine finished products to overseas or domestic win both markets. Then, the U.S. wine manufacturers' high delivery behavioral cost will impact to global wine consumers' desires to be fallen down because they will feel its sale price is not too reasonable high to reduce their wine consumption desires.

In conclusion, these three aspects of factors, which are every U.S. wine drinking product manufacturers need to consider before they achieve to do any kinds of wine businesses.

The other research considers U.S.alcohol consumption in U.S. and overseas markets. Alcohol is different to wine because some people feel alcohol, e.g. beer . It can hurt human's health, when the alcohol drinker often drinks beer. Otherwise, wine is health drinking product to global drinking consumers' feeling usually. So, U.S. alcohol manufacturers' consumers target will be limited to sell to the people who do not worry about any kinds of alcohol product , e.g. beer which can burt to their health. Unless, U.S. alcohol manufacturers can being good message to change the alcohol drinking consumers' attitudes to feel any alcohol products won't hurt whose health. Hence, U.S. alcohol manufacturers need have good methods to let global alcohol drinking consumers change to drink alcohol attitudes to let them to feel alcohol won't influence their health when they sometimes or often drink alcohol.

Hence, how to change their drinking alcohol habit to be accepted to drink alcohol behaviors which won't bring hurt to influence their health , this changing of drinking alcohol habit or attitude issue which will help any U.S. alcohol manufacturers to increase alcohol consumer number in long term. So, it is one valuable researching matter to any U.S. alcohol manufacturers. Moreover, it is valuable to underatand the trends and possible future patterns for alcohol consumption by beverage type given that the consumption of some alcoholic beverage types trends to have more strongly relationship with outcomes or actions that increase externality costs and negative health outcomes.

Also, U.S. alcohol manufacturers need to consider that every country's government charges how much alcohol taxes to import countries' alcohol manufactuers because any U.S. alcohol manufacturers will choose to raise higher alcohol sale price if the country government needs them to charge higher alcohol taxes to import t the country. Then, it will bring negative emotion influence to the high alcohol import tax country's alcohol consumers, due to the U.S. alcohol manufacturers charge higher sale price to their different kinds of alcohol products immediately. The sudden alcohol raising price factor will influence the high alcohol imported tax country's alcohol consumers feel any kinds of U.S. alcohol products won't be onre kind of health drinking product, due to their sale prices are raised suddenly. They will consume to drink othe kinds of U.S. drinking products, e.g. fruit juice, wine to replace U.S. alcohol drinking products. So, any U.S. similiar alcohol taste products will be the export alcohol drinking product manufacturers' competitors if the U.S. alcohol manufacturer's one alcohol imported country plans to raise 10 to 20%, even more alcohol imported tax to their alcohol products next month. Then, the imported alcohol country's alcohol consumer number will be caused to reduce more easily. Hence, any U.S. alcohol manufacturers need to consider when the import alcohol countries will raise alcohol imported tax to charge them in order to select other low alcohol imported tax or no raising imported tax countries to increase to export more alcohol products to them to replace the high tax countries alcohol imported to keep their competitive effort and build good brand to the U.S. alcohol manufacturers' image to the high alcohol imported tax countries' alcohol consumers to let them to feel the brand of U.S. alcohol manufacturer's alcohol is still valuable to select to buy to drink.

2.4 Apply (AI) technology improve US pork food logistic transportation speed in warehouse

Future , (AI) robotic machies can assist warehose workers to deliver the accurate pork food number and right weight to different locations in warehouses before they are delivered to different supermarkets or pork store sellers. Nowadays, pork ranks third in annual US meat consumption, behind beef and children averaging 51 pounds per person. US pork consumption varies by race and ethnitity. In general, US blacks race people consume 63 pounds of pork per person per year, whites race people 49 pounds and Hispanics 45 pounds. Otherwise, higher income US consumers tend to consume less pork.

Demographic data in the CSFII suggest future declines in per capita pork consumption, as increases of Hispanics and the elderly in US , who eat less port than the national average, enlarge their shared of the population. However, total US pork consumption will grow because of an expansion of the US population, e.g. US immigrants number will increase from different overseas.

In fact, although pork isn't consumed by certain populations or certain regions, it is one of the preferred meats in the world and United States. So, understanding the basic factor underlying pork consumption wil help US to supply in pork market and will able the meat industry to as well as it well the enable the industry (Economic research service, 2004).

In conclusion, US pork high income and white race consumers do not prefer to select pork to eat. it is possible due to they feel port is most common meat and purchase easily food. Hence, pork manufacturer (suppliers) ought raise pork sale quality and better taste, e.g. ungrade common pork from low meat quality and poor taste class meat to raise to high meat quality and better taste class meat to compare beef and sheep meet substitutes. Hence, building good public image to pork that is very importnt to influence US pork domestic consumption market, even overseas markets. This issue is all US pork suppliers need to consider if they expect to raise pork meat consumption effort in success in long term future.

• 31 •

CHAPTER THREE

Applying robots to improve tourism service performance

Future, predicting artificial intelligence (AI) and machine learning technology will be rapidly adopted for a range of application in the tourism entertainment industry. I shall explain how to apply (AI) to improve service performance for any kinds of financial service clients.

In the future, (AI) will be increased to supply to satisfy different kinds of tourism entertainment to satisfy whose needs to raise tourism service performance. The needs include: Tourism agents or airlines will use (AI) and machine learning methods to access air paper air ticket or electronic air ticket price to automate travelling client interaction. They are optimizing scarce capital will (AI) and machine learning techniques, as well as back-testing models and analyzing the tourism market impact of tourism entertainment need larger positions

Why and how (AI) and learning system can improve tourism service performance for any tourim institutions. The more efficient processing of information for example in travelling destiantion choice decisions and travelling customer interaction may contribute to a more efficient travelling destination choice system and it can help improve regulatory compliance and increase effectiveness. At the same time, network effects and scalability may give rise to third-party dependencies.

Applications of (AI) and machine learning can be variable to meet various financial institutions' needs. The uses of (AI) and machine learning will help tourism agent or airline institutions' clients to reduce personal or financial risk, e.g. data privacy, conduct risks. Also, adequate testing and training of tools with data and feedback mechanisms is important to ensure applications do what they are intended to do. So, (AI) and machine learning technology can be applied to financial industry as these aspects: customer -focused application, operation-focused uses application, trading and portfolio management application aspects.

(AI) big data is used broadly to storage and analysis of large and / or complicated data sets using a variety of techniques including (AI). The analytics often related to the amount of unstructured or sem-structured data in data sets. The technology can be applied to help any tourism agents or airline institutions to improve service performance. Machine learning may be defined aas a method of designing a sequence of actions to solve a problem, known as algorithms, which optimise automatically through experience and with limited or no human intervention. These techniques can be used find patterns in large amounts of data (big data analytics) from increasingly diverse and innovations sources to help any tourism or airline institutions for be supervised to learn to be improve service performance from every time the travelling client's tourism enterainment needs in any countries.

Why can (AI) deep learning algorithms be applied to tourism entertainment industry to raise service performance? For encoding the concept of a car case example, It is from a series of discovering generalisable concepts, such as encoding images. So, an investor might deploy an alogorithm to gather data to predict retail store sale numbers in a particular period. An alogorithm can recognise cars to count the number of cars in a retail parking lot of from a satellite image in order to infer a likely stores, sale figure for a particular period.

As applicationing to tourism entertainment service case, natural language processing of deep learning algorithms can allow computers to read and produce written text or when combined with voice recognition to read and produce spoken language to translate different countries language to let travellers to understand that the country can provide anywhere to let overseas travellers to go to its country to choose to travel . For financial loan case example, (AI) big data technology can also help financial institutions to decide whether the firm has ability to pay back loan and interest . When it borrow loan from the financial institution. This technology will help the financial institution to gather past data to evaluate and analyze its credit rate report more accurate than manual judgement. Even, it can help the financial institutions to evaluate how much loan amount can be lent to the firn more accurate in order to decide its loan pay back period and load and interest calculation amount to conclude the accurate lending loan service and interest charge amount to the firm (loan borrower) more confident.

Another example , it might be to automatically apply (AI) big data technology to read sale report or estimate an unrated company's intitial credit client's financial situation in order to evaluate whether the financial loan service firm has effort to pay its loan and interest to the financial company in the particular period in possib.e. Since cloud computing and internet technology created this new website technology can combine to (AI) deep learning algorithms.

In order to collect big amount, big data concerns the financial company's client's financial transactions in short time, e.g. big data on the scale of every single credit card transaction interconnectedness of information technology resources with cloud computing with whose big data can now be organized and analyzed. Using big data sets of this size and complexity and with the increase in cloud computing power, machine learning algorithms client's financial situation results more accurate than every financial consultant individual judgement.

In conclusion, human intelligence learning machine can replace or assist human financial consultants' some logic or complexity financial analysis tasks in any financial service organization's departments in order to reduce their workloads to achieve to improve financial service performance to their clients more satisfactory or effectively. Even future (AI) learning machine and big data and internet combination technology can bring these benefits to any financial service organizations, such as faster processor speeds, lower hardware cost, and better access to computer power via cloud computing services. If the financial service organization chose to apply (AI) machine learning technology to share financial service workers' tasks in different departments. It will bring to improve better service performance and reduce cost for the financial service organization in possible.

3.1 How to apply (AI) technology to improve service performance to satisfy US tourism consumers needs

Nowadays, tourism industry is every country's main leisure income. Every country will need have itself unique tourism features to attract travellers to go to travel easily. So, attractive unique tourism features can persuade different countrues travellers choose to go to itself country to travel more easily. I shall recommend what factors can influence global travelling consumers choose to go to US travel more easily. The travelling strategies can attempt to be implemented as below:

Firstly, US tourism leisure providers (travel agents) need to know what different countries' tourism consumers why and how to persuade them to feel US anywhere places are valuable to go to travel, what can attract them in these places, for Chinese travellers case example, what Chinese like to play when they choose to go to any one of the US domestic travelling placs. So, the US tourism leisure providers need to define the Chinese tourism consumers' tourism acts, attitude and travelling decisions regarding choosing, buying and consuming tourism products and tourism services and also its past consumer tourism reaction. Due to different countries' tourism consumers who have different tourism leisure needs, e.g. Chinese young age travellers prefer to choose to tourism package arrangement, who only like to buy air tickets and arrange their travelling journeys, e.g. they can choose where they will live and anywhere they choose to travel. So, US tourism service providers only concentrate on introducing anywhere US places valuable to let them to travel, calculating every journey transportation cost, and living and eating cost to let Chinese young tourism consumers to know. Otherwise, Chinese old age tourism consumers prefer to the US tourism service providers can arrange whole tourism journey to help them to reduce their worries about paying how much rent to live hotels, transportation costs in US anywhere journeys. Due to US is a large area country, many Chinese will feel worry about how to catch the bus, ferry, domestic air place, taxt, train , tram etc. transportation to go to any US domestic tourism places to pay the cheaper cost as well as how to find the reasonable price of hotels to live as well as how to choose the most valuable travelling places to travel and US anywhere touism places can be exciting and comfortable and enjoyable tourism leisure feeling in their whole US tourism journeys.

In special, the Chinese old age tourism consumers must consider above these challenges, they must need the US tourism leisure provider ensures to help them to arrange all their US tourism journey needs, then they will reduce worry to choose who is the best tourism leisure service provider if the US travel service provider can solve above all challenges for their US domestic journeys. So, the US doemstic tourism leisure arrangement service market competition is serious. Every US domestic tourism leisure provider needs have unique travelling leisure arrangement to attract them.

Secondly, US tourism service providers need to attempt to find different countries' tourism consumers' tourism leisure needs and how they make travelling journey decision processes because it can assist marketing manger to improve his/her own decision making process to forecast future different countries' tourism consumers' behaviors and to have a real and objective image of the country's general tourism consumer tourism leisure and tourism journey arrangement demands.

Hence, US tourism leisure service providers need to spend time to gather past different countries' tourism journeys arrangement tourism experience to develop new tourism products and services . It will include these questions for each country's travelling consumers' demands, such as below:

Who is important in the whole travelling journey arrangement decision making final tourism consumer?

What are the criteria every family or friend travelling group consumers' choice based on? e.g. travelling journey cost includes hotel, food, air ticket, leisure activities expenditure critera or how many days of the whole travelling journey criteria.

Where or when do they buy air ticket?

All these criteria will influence every tourism group consumer to make final travelling decision making to choose the US travelling servie provider or another one. Hence, when predicting travelling consumers buying processes, sometimes the travelling service provider will make false assumptions about these processes can result in an wrong assumption. Otherwise, good tourism journey arrangement product or service is not being bought. But, every time of making false assumption will raise the more accurate judgement effort to predict future every country's travelling consumers' journeys' arrangement and improve their travelling journey arrangement skill when their every time of false assumption. Hence, every US travel service provider won't need to fear fail to make false assumption. Otherwise, they need to revise every time false assumption in order to improve next time travelling jounrey arrangement service quality in order to raise their satisfactory level.

Thirdly, US travelling service providers need to understand what the factors can influence overseas travelling consumers' behavior. The factors include the personal factor, such as tourist's personality, self image, attitudes, motivations, perceptions, life style, age, family life style, profession. For example, if the travelling consultant felt the tourist, he/she likes to contact exciting things, then he/her travelling leisure will be the exciting travelling destinations, e.g. Walt Disney theme park, climing mountain sport, riding bicycles on hill sport, swimming sport, catching fast speed train transportation tool tourism journey arrangement. Otherwise, if the travelling consultant felt the tourist, he/she likes to contact quiet things, then his/her travelling leisure will be the quiet travelling destinations, e.g. walking around shopping centers, visiting book shops , walking on beaches etc. US cities or countryside walking travelling journey arrangement.

The another factor concerns the country's social culture, family, social class, reference groups. For example, Japanese social culture is common high social class to compare Chinese, Indian etc. So, their travelling demand will be higher to compare Chinese and Indian. For example, they like to eat better taste of food, when they choose to go ro anywhere to travel. So, US travellers need to arrange the better taste of food to eat. However, whether the US journey which have arrange Japan restaurant or Indian restaurant or Chinese restaurant to provide Japan food or Chinese food or India food taste to these countries travellers to eat. It is very important to influence any countries tourism consumers to choose to go to US to travel.

The other factor concerns situational factor, such as time, psychology, ambiance, social ambiance, state of mind. The country's good or bad social culture can influence travelling consumption motivation attitude. For example, when the country had good social culture to encourage the country's people to spend money to travel easily. So, this kind unconscious or conscious motivations are encouraged by the social culture to its living people. Then, its living people will be encouraged to select, organize and interpret sensory stimulation into a meaningful tourism picture of the world. So the country's good travelling leisure social culture will encourage the country's people to accept to spend money to go to anywhere for travelling leisure easily. It is one social tourism culture to encourage the country people to spend money to travel when they have holidays. So, any US tourism leisure service providers need to know what the country's social culture is in order to select the most suitable travelling destinations to attract them to travel to themselve America country more easily.

The other factor concerns age which is an effective discriminator of tourism consumer behavior. For example, young travellers have every different tourism tastes as regards travelling products or travelling trip service arrangement to compare to old travellers. Also, young age travellers tend to spend more than old age travellers. Thus, if the travelling service provider can predict what travelling needs of the old or young age traveller segments which can rise interest in tourism marketing from those tourism behavior point of view are: childhood , teenage, first youth, second youth and old age different tourism age segments' unique tourism leisure arrangement and tourism service and evaluate whether the travelling package price is the most reasonable to satisfy their different tourism age segments needs in order to evaluate the most reasonable travelling package price charge. Moreover, profession also has a great impact on tourism consumer behavior, profession young or old tourism segment and non-profession young or old tourism segment, due to their education level has high or low difference. So, its impact over an individual tourism decision is obvious difference. For example, professional young or old age travellers can have more money to spend high class expensive tourism leisure. So, tourism journey arrangement can be belonged to a medium or high class. They usually demand high rates accomodation and meal and expensive train, air plane, ferry etc. transport tools in their auxiliary services during the journey. Otherwise, non-professional young or old age travellers can not have enough money to spend high class expensive tourism leisure. So , tourism journey arrangement can be belonged to a low class. They usually demand low rates accomodation and meal and cheap tram, train , air plane, ferry etc. transportion tools in their poor services during the journey.

Thus, US tourism firms will need have interest in attracting opinion leader because their abilities to influene groups and try to convince them regarding the tourism service quality of their tourism service needs.

The final factor concerns economic factor. It is the most sensitive to environmental change and it is as a result, US tourism service providers have been very affected by the global economic situation influence.

In the past, tourism plays an important role in the European economy. Many labor were dominated by this tourism industry, due to global number of visitors has been increasing fastly in the past between ten to twenty years. Thus, the global economy is influenced to recovery, being influenced by economies from Asia and America which register continued and considerable increases.

As Europe tourism industry case,many countries implemented domestic tourism visitor number measures, delaying the economic recovery perspectives, already weak. The euro and American dollar, but the possibilities tourist from all over the world, with of special offers and low price vacations. Thus, economic factor influences dollar exchange change which will also influence global travellers choose whether they ought need choose Asia or Europe or America to travel by exchange dollar variable factor influence.

Hence, US tourism leisure service providers need to concernn global economic environment how will change in order to make solutions to avoid global travellers choose to go to Asia or Europe or America to travel, due to these countries' money exchange rate can bring beneficial to let them to spend less than choice to go to US travel. So, it implies that economic changing behavior can influence global tourism consumers to choose to go to America to travel, even their earlier tourism country is US.

In conclusion, all these factors will influence global travellers' tourism countries choices and tourism leisure activities and tourism journey arrangement choices serious. Thus, US tourism leisure providers need to consider global economy will how change and discover many different kinds of tourism leisure arrangement package in order to arrange the different kinds of the most suitable tourism leisure package to satisfy global tourism consumers' unique tourism leisure consumer segments' needs.

• 41 •

CHAPTER FOUR

Can robots raise productive efficiency in industrial sector

When (AI) robotic technology is applied to any industrial sectors, instead of replacing or helping labor workers to do some simple tasks to share their workload beneficial aspect, whether it can really help them to raise productivity growth or work efficiency in any industrial working environments. Which are subindustries the most strongly affected by the automation potential of (AI)? How can managers of industrial players cooperate with (AI) and workers work efficiently in order to achieve to raise productivity growth aim?

Future (AI) technology can bring two aspects of benefits in industrial sector manufacturing operations and business processes both aspects as below:

On manufacturing operations aspect, predictive maintenance is enhanced by (AI) allows for better prediction and avoidance of machine failure by combining data from advanced internet of things (IOT) sensors and maintenance logs as well as external sources. So, asset productivity can increase of up to 20% are possible , and overall maintenance costs may be reduced up to 10%; collaborative aware robots will improve production through based on (AI) enabled human machine interaction in labor-intensive settings. Therefore, productivity increases up to 20% are feasible for certain-tasks, even when tasks are not fully automatable; yield enhanccement in manufacturing powered by (AI) will result in decreased scrap rates are testing costs by linking various across machinery groups and sub-processes, e.g. in the semi-conductor industry, the use of (AI) can lead to a reduction in yield detraction by up to 30%. Moreover, automated quality testing can be realized using (AI). By employing advanced image recognition techniques for visual inspection and fault detections productivity increases of up to 50% are possible. Specificantly, (AI) based visual inspection based on image recognition may increase defect detection rates up to 90% as compared to human inspection.

On business processes beneficial aspect, (AI) enhanced supply chain management greatly improves forecasting accuracy when increasing and optimizing stock replenishment. Reductions between 20 and 50% in forecasting errors are feasible. So, lost sales due to products not being available can be reduced by up to 65% and inventory reductions of 20% to 50% are achieved; The application of machine learning to enable high-performance R&D projects has large potential. So, research and research cost reductions of 10 to 15% and time-do-market improvements up to 10% are expected. Finally, business support function automation will ensure improvements in both process quality and efficiency. Automation rates of 30% are possible across functions. For the specific example IT service desks, automation rates of 90% are expected.

Can (AI) automatin technology innovate the future of production? Trends towards higher levels of automation causes greater speed and precision of producton as well as reduced exposure to dangerous tasks for employees. New production technologies could help overcome the stagnant productivity and make may for more valued added activity in production sector.

Exciting advances in the internet of things, artificial intelligence, advanced robotics, wearables and 3 D printint are transforming what, where and how products are designed, manufactured, assembled, distributed, consumed, service after purchase, even reused. They affect and alter all end-to-end steps of the production process and as a result, transform the products that consumers demand, the factory process and the management of global supply chains, addition to industry pecking orders and countries' access. So, future (AI) robotic technology will be applied to those production sectors. They include 80% of wearables market and almost 70% of industrial 3D printing units. Other specific industries with automotive, electronics and aerospace being early adopter in most cases to apply (AI) robotic technology to help their workers to work more efficient and to achieve productivity growth.

In fact, competitive production is demanded to reduce cost in higher manufacturing cost environmeents. (AI) robotic technology will have possible to help manufacturers to reduce cost, e.g. when the production environment occurs in the capital-intensive sectors with high transportation costs . So, if the manufacturer does not choose to apply (AI) robotic manufacturing technology to help it to assist workers to manufacture in factory. Then, it's traditional manufacturing technology will negatively impact white and blue-collar workers on the factory floor if societies do not ready their workforce for the new (AI) robotic skill sets and put in place transition mechanisms to ease negative impacts.

Future, (AI) robotic technology will bring these advantages to manufacturing industry's production process: Mapping a comprenhensive technology to impact one or more aspects of global production systems. Exercises followed to prioritize and focus analysis on deemed to have the broadest applicability across value chain elements; a foresight series was created for each production (AI) robotic technology. Capturing current technical readiness and adoption levels across (AI) robotic production processes, manufacturing industries focusing on the impact of the (AI) robotic production technologies by understanding the connections between (AI) robotic manufacturing technology and traditional non-(AI) robotic manufacturing technology and they compete in solving firm by social production process problems and by bringing the positive production method impact on the factory floor and on firms, industries, societies and individual manufacturing needs.

For example, advanced robotics can be applied to 3 D printing technological manufacturing copied product tasks from digital -physical transformation. So, (AI) robotics can replace workers to do any 3D printing tasks to copy any products. The benefits to change the factory's physical location to be small areas, high speed network, raising producers' revenues (new offering, business models) and reducing cots (selling, administrative expenses, logistic etc.) , less long term investments and capabilities to achieve 3 D printing product increasing number in efficient (AI) robotic working speed. Although , it is possible to destroy factory labor worker 3 D printing product job, but it can create new 3 D printing (AI) robotic controller working jobs to be technicians to teach (AI) robotic machines to learn how to use 3 D printer to manufacture any copied products. The most important benefit of 3D robotic machines replacing labor 3D printing labors that is the manufacturer can reduce labor 3 D printing worker number, due to the manufacturer applies (AI) robotic to assist the 3D printing workers to fo every step of manufacturing copied product tasks. So, the 3D printing (AI) robotic machine labors can replace all 3 D printing labor workers to do every step to apply 3 D printers to manufacture every copied product. Otherwis, the 3 D printing copied product manufacture will employ the (AI) robotic technicians to control and supervise and teach the (AI) robotic 3 D printing product machines to learn how to use the 3 D printers to do every step to manufacture different kinds of copied products to sell in the market. Hence, the 3 D printer copied product manufacture will reduce labors and salary when it applies 3 D printing robotic machine labors to replace labor workers to finish every printing step to manufacture different kinds of copied products in factory. for example, when the 3 D printing technicians had taught the robotic machine to learn how to apply 3 D printer to manufacture a copied vehicle's motor engine. Then, the (AI) robotic machine had learnt how to apply the 3D printer to manufacture different kinds of copied vehicle motor engines in every step. It is possible that the (AI) robotic machine 3D printing skills will be improved more better to compare human 3 D printing workers' skills as well as its 3D printing vehicle motor engine copied product manufacturing speed will also faster than human 3D printing worker's printing copied manufacturing product's speed. Consequently, it will bring positive benefits to any kinds of vehicle engine products productivity number growth to sell different kinds of vehicle engines to vehicle sellers to different country vehicle sale market in order to raise its global vehicle engine sale market competitive effirt and revenue. So, (AI) robotic machine seems really raise productivity growth when it is applied to manufacturing industry.

Why is (AI) learning system the best tool to be applied to manufacturing industry? In fact, future (AI) robotic machine will be one kind of intangible capital to manufacturing organizations to help them to innovate, adjustment costs, organizational changes to be better and new manufacturing skills are needed for successful in every production process.

Historically, most computer programs were created by codifying human knowledge, step-by-step, mapping inputs to outputs by the programmers. In constrast, machine learning systems use categories of general algorithms , e.g. neural networks to figure out the relevant mapping on their own, typically by being fed very large data sets of examples. By using these machine learning methods bring the growth in total data and data processing resources, machines have made impressive gains in perception and cognition, two essential skills for most types of human work.

Nowadays, an increasing number of companies have responded to these high technological opportunities to be applied to manufacturing function aspect, such as Google now describes its focus on " AI first", when Microsoft's CEO says (AI) is the " ultimate breakthrough" in technology. Their optimism about (AI) is not just cheap talk. They are making heavy investments to apply (AI) technology in manufacturing function aspect. The possibility is that the gains of (AI) manufacturing function new technologies are already attainable to different kinds of manufacturing industries. Assuming the (AI) robotic manufacturing worker technologies are at least partially rivalrous. Their effect on averge productivity growth is modest overall, and is virtually not essential need fo median worker. For instance, two of the most profitable uses of (AI) for targeting and pricing online ads. and for automated trading of financial instruments, both applications with many zero-sum aspects.

Hence, I predict that future one day will occur many low skillful level workers lose their manufacturing jobs in factories, due to many manufacturing firms choose to apply (AI) robotic machines to replace human labor workers to help them to manufacture any products in order to achieve increasing productivity growth and reducing manufacturing labor number and wages and raising revenue aims. It is really a good reason to be optimistic about the future productivity growth potential of new technologies, such as (AI) robotic machine to be replaced to the traditional slow speed and low efficient productivity and high cost manufacturing method or technique to any factories.

In conclusion, due to manufacturers expect to raise productivity growth aim. It has two main sources of the delay between recognition of a new technology, such as (AI) robotic machine's potential and its measurable effects. One is that it takes time to build the stock in the new technology to a size sufficient enough to have an aggregate effect. The other is that complementary investments are necessary to obtain the full benefit of the new technology, such as (AI) robotic manufacturing technology and it takes time to discover and develop these complements and to implement them. When, the fundamental importance of the core invention and its potential for society might be clearly recognizable at the outset, the myriad necessary co-invention, obstacles and adjustment needed along the way award discovery over time if future one day had another kind new manufacturing technology which can replace (AI) robotic manufacturing method to be better.

Hence, it explains that futuer there are many manufacturing industries choose to apply (AI) robotic machines to replace human workers in factory manufacturing environments in order to achieve the raising of productivity growth in efficient way aim more easily.

4.1 Apply (AI) technology to raise US lighting product productivity growth

Future, (AI) robotic machines can help warehouse workers to apply 3D printers to manufacture any copied different kinds of lighting products to raise productivity growth to satisfy different lighting design consumers needs in efficient way and fast manufacturing speed to manufacture different kinds of design lighting products to satisfy different lighting home and shopping center customers' needs. Every country has itself lighting market customer characterization because different lighting products have different types, functions, colors, designs to attract lighting customer choice. Lighting consumers functions include home reading room, dinner room, bed room, toilet function; office lighting working environment function; shopping center shopping environment functionl transportation tools driving at night etc. different light functions.

What are US lighting product unique characterizations? In US future lighting consumption market. Its lighting products will be focused on their unique advantages to beneficial any lighting consumers. US lighting product manufacturers will need to implement technological research such as: lighting energy saving technology. Energy saving is consumed by light sources in US, lighting technologies how many are installed, where they are installed, the performance attributes are of the installed stock of lighting technologies. So, future US lighting product is needed energy saving technology to help lighting consumers to reduce electricity expenditure at residential, commercial and industrial places for office, home, education, retail, public or private car driving light etc. different light needs. So, effective lighting energy saving technology will help public and business and personnel lighting users to reduce much electricity expenditure. So, lighting energy saving technology will be the most importnt factor to influence future potential light consumers to choose to buy the lighting product manufacturer's any lighting products to compare attractive design, style, shape, color , size light product appearance factors. Because in general, any lighting product consumers will like any lighting products can spend less electricity in order to reduce electricity expenditure when they use every day.

Hence, future US key elements of lighting product sale successful factor, any US lighting product sale market will need have these elements, such as: quantity, type, application, and energy use of stationary lighting in the US. Performance characteristics of lighting technologies, trends, drivers and barriers to improved efficiency in the lighting market. Opportunities for energy savings through advances in lighting technology and adoption of best practices, overview of ongoing lighting research in the public and private sectors. It is not only only for lighting product sale in US domestic sale market. It is also included to lighting products export overseas market. Because global lighting product consumers consider how to consume less electricity to use lighting product in order to save electricity energy and expenditure. So, lighting energy -saving technology is value consideration to any US lighting product manufacturers in the future lighting sale market development.

Who will be US future energy -saving lighting product consumption target? I shall indicate as below: Residential consumption target can include manufactured residential , family manufactured business, lighting product consumer who needs lighting product to in their family factory, so they expect to spend less electricity for lighting expenditure in those family manufacturing proceed. Residential single family and multi-family either less than 4 units or 4 or more units, who needs lighting product when they have need to bath or eat dinner or read ot watch television any indoor activities when they are living in their residential homes at night. So, they also expect to buy energy-saving lighting products to reduce their electricity consumption expenditure. Another lighting product consumers are commercial lighting users. This commercial lighting consumer number will be large and their lighting electricity needs will also be much, due to they use light for commercial functions. Such as vacant, office/professional, laboratory, warehouse/non-refrigerated, food sales, public order/safety, health care (out patient) , warehouse (refrigerated), public assembly, religious worship, education, food service, health care (inpatient), hospital ward room patient light service, surgeon room medical surgeon light function , hotel/motel/dorm room light function, shopping mall/center light function for shopping customers, retail shops, excluding shopping mall lighting function etc. different commercial functions. So, lighting commercial customers number and their light needs will be more, due to commercial clients need to turn on lighting products in their stores or hospitals or warehouses etc. different indoor places to use in all days in possible.

Otherwise, residential family lighting users will only use light at night , due to who need to leave their homes to go to offices to work or go to schools to study. So, they will stay at house at night in common. Even, if they stay at homes in the morning or afternoon. They won't need to use lighting at this sunny time. So, residential light consumers will only use lighting product at night in common. Also, it will influence their demand of lighting products' design, color, energy -saving function. Their demand won't be very high. Otherwise, commercial lighting product consumers, they will often need light to help them to serve their clients or serve themselves in offices, hospitals, warehouses, schools, hotels, shopping malls (centers) etc. different places. So, this often useful functions influence their lighting products' design, type, color, what manufacturing materiall is used and the most important need is energy-saving demand, due to the light consumers can save more money to use lesser electricity. So, their lighting product demands are higher to compare residential lighting product consumers. This issue is US lighting product manufacturers need to consider before they decide how to manufacture any lighting products to sell to US domestic or export to overseas lighting market.

The final light consumer target is industrial consumption users. I believe that they will be the most need of light consumers. Because they will need light working environment to help their workers to work ot manufacture any products in factories. The industrial consumers include food product manufacturers, tobacco product manufacturers, textile mill product manufacturers , appear and other textile product manufacturers, apparel and other textile product manufacturers, lumber and wood product manufacturers, furniture and fixtures product manufacturers, paper and allied product manufacturers, printing and publishing product manfacturers, chemicals and allied product manufacturers, petroleum and coal product manufacturers, rubber and miscellaneous plastics product manufacturers, leather and store, glass product manufactuers , primary metal industries manufacturers, fabricated metal product manufactuers, industrial machinery and equipment product manufacturers , electronic and electric equipment manufacturers, transportation equipment manufacturers. Due to they need many workers to help them to manufacture any products in factories. So, enough light environment is important to influence their productivities and efficiencies. So , they will need to buy many lighting products to assist their workers to work anywhere in factories. So, anywhere in factories will need much light to let workers to feel comfortable and visable . So, this industrial light consumers target will be the lighting product's main consumers because they must need to buy many lighting products to let their workers to work in enough light factory environment, even if any lighting products are damaged or used to long time, they will buy other better quality new lighting products to replace these any one of damaged or old lighting products.

In conclusion, it seems that industrial lighting customer number ought be the highest and their demand to lighting products' light quality , such as reducing the lowest dark environment, energy-saving function, lighting products' safety and lighting products' durable and even reasonable price demand which will be the most top to compare othe kinds of lighting product consumers in US , even overseas export lighting market. All US lighting manufacturers ought need to concern how to design the attractive different kinds of lighting product styles to satisfy whese different kinds of lighting product consumers' needs, instead of design aspect, energy-saving technology, light solor, size, reasonable price etc. different factors will influence lighting consumer number.

Reference

Economic research service, factors affecting US pork consumption, 2004

Economic research service, USDA ,U.S. Department Of Agriculture Economic Research Service (ERS)

Girod, B. and De Haan P 2010 More or letter ? A model for changes in household greenhouse gas emissions due to higher income J. Indust. Ecol. 14 31-49.

Meinshauen M et al 2011. The RCP greenhouse gas concentrations and their extensions from 1765 to 2300 clim._change 109 213-41.

Palley Thomas I. 2002 " Economic contradictions coming home to roost? Does the U.S. economy face a long-term aggregate demand generation problem? Journal of post Keynesian Economics, Fall 2002, vol. 25 no. 19

Setterfield , mark, 2010, " Real wages , aggregate demand and the macroeconomic travails of the U.S. economy. Diagnosis and prognosis. " Trinity college department of economic working paper 10-05.

State of the plate , 2015. study on America's consumption of fruit and vegetables, product for better helth foundation, U.S.

Van Ruijven B. De Vries B. Van Vuuren DP and Van Der Sluijs, JP 2010 . A global model for residential energy use: uncertainty in calibration to regional data energy 35 269-82.

CHAPTER FIVE

Can robots improve performance

Human Behavioral network job brings social economic benefits

What does human network job mean ? Why may human network job be popular? Why human network job behavior may influence economy ?

Nowadays internet is popular to use. We can apply internet to find data , search any new things, even earn money. Why does internet may become huma network job source. For example, e-publish may be one kind of new human network job. Any authors may apply internet

channel to help them to sell electronic or paper books from e-publisher web store. They may apply facebook, you tub etc. any online

channel to promote themselves new books to let new readers to know whether when they may buy themselves favourable new topic books to read

from electronic publisher web store.

Thus, future electronic publisher industry may help any authors to build internet network platform to help them to sell and promote ot advertise their any one new electronic or paper book topic to let global any one reader to choose to buy their any new topic books from electronic publisher web store easily and conveniently. However, it implies that electronic network platform author may be one kind of future new human network job in our societies.

How electronic network platform author job may bring economy benefit in macro economy view? A person can have few friends, contacts and still be very influential if these few

friends and contacts are themselves highly influential, e.g. one author must not need to know any one reader in global society. When they like to choose any electronic books from electronic internet network platform. They may become the author's any one topic book buyer, when they feel the author's any one topic book is fun and attract they make decision to buth the strange author whose the topic book from electronic book publisher's platform web store conventiently in short time. Although, they are strangers, they do not know themselves , but the reader can understand what it way that made Google from writing platofrm to create new creative mind and typing network job method to replace traditional hand writing book method for global authors. It will be one kind of new human network writing job.

Hence, global any one reader can apply an innovative search engine , such as google.com to find whether whom author personal new topic books are value to read from internet.

Then, the electroniuc publisher's web store may be new book store platform sale network to help the author to sell many electronic or paper books from electronic network platform

in short time. So, internet may be future new network plaform to help global any one author to create network writing job absolutely. Furthermore, internet may be popular social media

to help any one author to build goold relationship between his/ her readers. It is one kind of new network, human network job. New authors do not need to buy many paper books to prepare to put in any one book shop warehouse. Their every book can print on demand to reduce out of book stock in any one book shop. They may choose to sell either electronic books or paper books both from any one book publisher web store. So, electronic network platform may be one kind of good writing channel to help human authors to create income and it can also help authors to bring new creative mind and new topic fun content books to let readers to know and buy to read from electronic publisher network platform.

Why does human behavior may be one kind of new human network job to bring global economic advantages. ALthough, it may be free income or without inocme, but the person does the network behavior, his/her behavior may be bring advantages to influence many other people's health. For this case, when a worker in a coffee shop in an airport gets a vaccination aganinst the flu, it does not only helps him or her stay healthy, but also helps the many travellers who might otherwise have been inflected if that workers caught the flu. So, the externality , the result implies the vaccination of even a part of a community conveys benefits to the whole community. For example, governments pay special attention to the vaccinations of school children, teachers, health mothers, and the elderly, categories of people particularly susceptible not only to catching, but also to transmitting a disease.

It is not accidental that governments are heavily involved with vaccination . When there are externalities, free market, fail to persuade individual incentives with society's
their the worker's decision of whether to get a vaccine ends up attracting whether other people get sick. The workers might not fully take all these other people's potential suffering into account when making her or his vaccination decision.

As Stanford University does many suggestions, understand this and tries to help them make the right decisions and so providers free flu vaccines for its staff and students.
Small pockets of unvaccinated individuals can allow a disease to gain a spread more widely well-being. For example, parent weighing the costs and benefits of a vaccine for their child is not always thinking of the consequences of that vaccination to other people. THese are markets in which subsidizing or regulating behavior can make everyone better off. Because the reason for requiring that a child be vaccinated before enrolling in school is not just to protect that child, because each child's vaccination affects others via potential contagions.

Robots take our jobs behavioral and economy influences
Robot job behavior brings economy influences

If one day robots can replace human to do simple, even complex jobs. They will bring what influences to our global societial economy.The popular economic refrain declares that the
global middle class is dying and robots will soon take our jobs, e.g. shopping center customer service jobs, library service jobs, cinema ticket sale jobs, restaurant kitchen cooker jobs,
even, bus drivers, taxi drivers etc. public transport driving jobs, accountant, doctors etc. professional jobs. Whether it is beautiful or petty matter if our future societies have many human jobs can be replaced to do from robots. Businessman must may reduce to employ employees and reduce to pay salary or wage, when robots can be replaced to do their employees tasks. But, societies must bring unemployement rate rises , due to societies will have many people loss jobs when their employers choose to buy robots to serve their clients or do any office tasks or customer service or cleaning etc. tasks.

In micro economy view, employers may save money in long term, but in macro economy view, it will cause unemployment ratio rises , even crime rate rises when there are many people lose
jobs in societies. These models of doom, though, fail to account for the hundreds of businesses riding the waves of change in their industries when robots may be invented to replace human to do many simple , even complex tasks in our future societies.

WE may image that one small factory needs to manufacture fishes canes to sell to supermarket, the small , cheaper stuff and higher margin parts of the fishes manufacture industry. Before, this factory needs to employe many human factory workers need to help every fresh customer makeing the perfect fishing gear, designed for performance, durability, and cost in order to achieve to manufacture every fish cane in whole fished processing manufacturing stages. Every worker needs to spend about 15 to twenty minutes to finish every fish cane , till to delivery to any supermarket to sell. If this fish canes manufacturing factory can apply manufacturing robots to help them to finish any one working tasks , every robot can only spend five minutes to finish whole fresh fish cane manufacturing process. Thus, every robot can

help this factory save 10 to 15 minutes time to finsh every fish cane manufacturing process. IN fact, time is money, because when every robot can help this factory to reduce 10 to 15 minutes time to compare human worker. Then, this factory can finish about 20 fish canes in one hour if it can use robot to help it to manufacture fish canes. Otherwise, if this factory still use human workers to help it to manufacture fish canes, then it can finsh about 3 to 4 fish canes in one hour. SO, the manufacturing efficiency ensures that robots must help this fish manufacturing factory to raise fish canes number more than human workers. So, in robotic behavioral economy view, manufacturing robots must help this fish canes manufacturing factory to raise fish canes manufacturing number and deliver increasing number to supermarkets to prepare to sell every day. Robots can help this fish canes manufacturing factory bring manufacturing time saving, rising manufacturing efficiency, improving performance and reducing wages expenditure long time advantages in micro economy view. However, manufacturing robots can also bring disadvanages to society, e.g. increasing unemployment ratio, increasing crime rate,

this factory workers will lose jobs and income, they need earn social welfare from government and increasing government finance pressure in short time, even long time in macro economic view.

Stanford University graduate program in economics, Scott lecturer explained that "in demand and supply economic theory for robots supply and demand case, robots supply number increasing may influence human workers demand number decrease. It sometimes calls " the efficient frontier".

No specific human beings were mentioned in any of economics classes. As robots supply and demand in market case, They (robots) may be purely theoretical " agents" who reached to the most reasonable sale prices in order to persuade any one businessman buyer to make manufacturing robot buying decision whether robots can help him / her to bring how much saving time , saving money, saving cost, improving performance, efficiency economic benefit before he/she plans to reduce workers number when he/she decides to apply robots to replace human workers in his/her factory or office or any service department, e.g. cinema ticket sale service, shopping center customer service, shopping center cleaning , supermarket customer service etc. service or sale tasks. When robots can replace human to do any one of these tasks in any organizations. So, robots may be human worker agents who reached to prices the way robots would react to a software

command. There was nothing that explained why some people thrived and others did n't or why truly brilliant, hardworking people could fail when much lazier folks succeeded." Having been admitted to the Stanford University graduate program in economics, Scott lecturer hoped to get his answers there.

How robots influence our future social changing? Using the right technology can be a boon to your business in this economy. For internet example, it is easier than ever to find well-matched customers all around the world, to stay in contact with them, and to more quickly design the products they want. If you focus solely on being cutting -edge, though you risk letting the technology

take over what should be very robust relationships with your customers , employees, and colleagues. IN nowaddays society, technoligical advances and cutomation, personal

relationships in business are more crucial than ever. I mean that robots can not replace human to serve clients to let them to feel more comfortable and passion more easily. For shoe shop case example, if the shoe shop apply one robot to serve its clients to replace human shoe salesperson to serve its shoe customers. Robots ensure that they can not persuade every shoe potential buyer to make shoe buying decision more easily when robots need to contact every shoe potential buyer. The reason is simple, because robots can not touch any one shoe buyer individual emotion very easier. If the shoe buyer needs the robots to help him/her to choose any right shoe styles when he/she can not feel himself / herself can make the most right shoe style choice decision. The robots can not replace human shoe salesperson to make shoe style choice judgement more easily. They must need longer time to analyze whether which shoe style may be the most suitable to the shoe buyer. Otherwise, human shoe salesperson may attempt to make the most right shoe style choice decision to help any one shoe buyer to chooce the most right style shoe because he/she owns shoe style sale experience, shoe style knowledge, the most important reason is that they can feel every shoe customer individual emotion to touch whether he/she will feel comfortable or happy when they attempt to help every shoe customer to seek the most right shoe style in every shoe customer whole shoe searching processing. Othwerwise, serving robots are only one machine, they can not touch or feel every shoe customer individual emotion whether he/she feel comfortable or unhappy or happy when they need to contact them in whole shoe searching processing. Hence, I believe that some tasks robots can

not repalce human staff to do very easily. Otherwise, robots may bring disadvanatges to let any one businessman to loss his/her customers, due to robots can not touch every customer

emotion to compare human staff in service tasks more easily. Robots serving customer behaviors may cause money lose and customers number lose to the shop in micro economic view.

Intellectual human economic behaviors

What does intellectual human economic behaviors mean ? I believe that when we choose or decide to do intellectual behaviors, then our societies will be influenced to bring economic growth in consequence.I shall attempt to indicate pollution case to explain how and why eithet our intellectual or foolish behaviors may bring economic growth or recession in consequence as below:

On one hand, for air pollution social case aspect example, if we only consider to buy cars to drive for working aimr or holiday leisure aim. Then, our societies air will be polluted. Our health will be influenced to bad. Our car driving behaviors may cause global environment air pollution serously. In long tiem, global air pollution will bring our bodies health to be bad. Although, ourselves car driving behaviors may bring our driving travelling leisure enjoyment and comfortable feeling in short time, also we so not need to pay public transport fare often, but we need to compensate ourselves health economic intangible loss due to air pollution , when cars number increases, dirty air will cause ouselves health to become bad.

In the result, we will need to pay more medical expenditure when we are old age, due to ourselves bodies will become bad, due to we breathe global dirty air every day, due to ourselves cars pollute air in long time, e.g. 10 to 20 years, even 30 more without limited air pollution environment. So, driving cars behavior may be one kind of human foolish behavior and our foolish behavior may bring ourselves future long time medical expenditure absolutely.

One the other hand, water pollution social aspect, if we often keep much rubblish to pollute sea, oil exploration porcessing pollute ocean , ships gas pollute ocaen, then fishes will eat polluted food and drive dirty water, due to global ocean is polluted.

In fact, because human only to conside how to buy boats to carry on leisure enjoyment activities, or catch cruises to travel on the sea. Also, oil manufacturers only consider researching anywhere to find new oil exploration places to manufacture oil product, when their oil exploration processes pollute ocarn . Consequently, global fishes drink polluted warer or eat polluted food. They will have poison. SO, human will have high chance to eat poison polluted fishes, due to fishes are poison or are polluted.

So, human is doing foolish activities, we only hope to find oil exploration places to pollute ocean or we only spend money to buy ticket to catch ships to travel anywhere in global ocean. All of these human foolish behaviors will bring pollution to global ocean. On consequently, we will need to compensate to eat polluted or dirty or poision fishes, ourselves bodies health will be bad. In long time, we need have high chance to pay medical expenditure when we are old. So, pollution case may be one good example to explain how and why human foolish behavior may influence ourselves future need to compensate serious medical loss.

All of these human foolish behavior will bring pollution to global ocean. On consequently, we will need to compensate to eat polluted or dirty or poison fished , ourselves bodies health will be bad. In long time, we will have high chance to pay medical expenditure, when we are old. So, pollution case may be one good example to explain how and why human ourselves intellectual or foolish behaviors may influence future long time economic loss or economic growth or recession in micro and micro economic view.

On another water pollution aspect hand, if we often keep rubbish to sea, oil exploration processing pollutes ocean and ships' gas pollute ocean, then fishes will eat polluted food and drink dirty water, due to fishes will eat polluted food and drink dirty sea water because the global ocean is polluted seriously.

In fact, because human only consider how to buy boats to carry on any leisure water activities, or catches cruises to travel on the sea. Also, oil manufacturers only consider any where to find oil exploratin places to manufacture oil products from ocean, when their pol exploration processes can plooute ocean. Consequently, global fishes drink polluted water or eat direty food. They will have poison. So, human will have high chance to eat poison fishes.

Otherwise, such as pollutin case, it can infuence inflation or deflation. Consequently, the reason indicates supply and demand theory. If air pollution is serious, then we will consider health issue, global cars demand number may be influenced to reduce, when global cars number demand will reduce, global car prices and supply number will need to change to fall down in order to attract or persuade global car consumers choose to make car purchase decision.

Hence, global car manufacture number and car price will be influenced to reduce, due to global air pollution issue. Consequently, deflation will occur because when the country citizen usually does not spend much extra saving money to buy car expensive goods. Money value will be low. Otherwise, if global cair pollution is not serious, human considers to buy cars to enjoy driving leisure lives. So, global car demand is influenced to increase , also global car price will also influenced to increase.

Consequently, gobal human will choose to buy cars to drive. Due to we accept to spend extra saving to buy expensive car goods. Car sale price and supply may be influenced to rise up. Money value is influenced to reduce. Inflation may be influenced, due to global car consumers number increases, we would not have extra money to spend easily. Car expensive goods expenditure influences our spending habit to avoid to make car purchase decision more easily. So, human intellectual or foolish activities may bring inflation or deflation consequency in possible indirectly in macro economic view.

On conclusion, above pollution case explain that how and why human intellectual or foolish economic behaviors may bring inflation or deflation consequency as wll as economic growth or recession consequency as well as any goods demand and supply increasing or decreasing consequency. It implies that human behavior may have indirect relationship to influence any goods demand and supply number to either increase or decrease result as well as any goods price will be influenced to increase or decrease in micro and macro economic view.

The relationship between social change and human behavior

Why does economic changes may influence human individual behavioral change? I shall attempt to indicate shopping behavior and staying at home behavior to explain their case and effect relationsip as below:

Human behavior can be influenced by economic change or economic change can be influenced by human behavior? Why does recession may influence consumers reduce shopping desire? In social recession suitation, it is possible that many people lose jobs suddenly, due to businessmen lose many customers. They need to make decision to reduce employees number in order to continue to keep businesses. Consequently, many firms (organizations) their employees may lose jobs. When they have much time, due to lose jobs, they will feel to avoid to spend too much time and money to go to shopping often. Many losing jobs people, they will often stay at homes.

So, they will reduce time to go to shopping, then non essential products won't their preferable choice purchase products. Hence, recession will change many losing jobs people their shopping or consumption desires to avoid to buy non essential products often . Usually when economic boom, many people have jobs to do because consumers number must increase when many people have jobs to do. Then, many people can accept to spend money to buy non essential products often. Many people feel spend time to go to shopping can satisfy their purchase of any kinds of new products useful psychology or desire. So, recession is one good example to explain it can influence many people do not like often to leave homes to go to shopping easily. Many people like to stay at homes, becaue they feel worry about spending too much shopping time when they leave homes. Their staying home time is one good negative shopping behavior example. So, economic change may influence human individual behavior changes , they have direct cause and efect relationship in behavioral economic view.

May human behavior influence economic change? Is it possible that human behavior may bring the country social economic change in macro economic or micro behavioral economic view ? I shall indicate publishing industry example. Do you feel that if there are many students feel learning is very important when they read many books or many of students feel interesting to read or they have reading new books in habit, then it is possible that the country will have many students like to spend time to go to any book shops to choose the books, they feel that they can help they learn new knowledge. Then the country will increase students number, they often spend time to visit any one book shop every week. Their visiting book shops behavior which may become their habits. So, the country will increase students number, they often spend time to visit book shops. Also, it implies that visiting book shops behaviors may be their behavioral habits.

So, when the country has many students often spend time to visit book shops , their visiting book shops behaviors may help any one book shop to raise books sale chance. So, the country's student individual often visiting book shop behaviors, their habitual visiting book shops behaviors must may assist help any one book shop to increase books sale number absolutely.

Consequently, any one book shop , its books sale bumber must be influenced to increase to increase because the country will have many students like or feel need visit book shops habit in order to choose any suitable books to buy to read at home in order to raise themselves learning effort. When the country has many bok shops often have many students visit their book shops, then their books sale number may be influenced to increase. It explain why student individual visiting book shop behavior may help any one book shop sale number increases also.

How human productive behavior may influence economic development

May any country which citizen behavior assist themselves country development? It is one cause and effect economic question. I mean that if the country itself citicen can not concentrate mind or energy to choose to do one kind of industry in order to let themselves country can bring the most benefit, then whether the counry itself economy can bring the most serious economic benefit. I shall attempt to indicate these countries themselves indistry choice to explain whether these countries themselves citizen productive behavior may help themselves countries to achieve the largest economic benefits. I shall indicate as below:

New Zealand farmer individual wine productive behavior

For New Zealand country example, this country concerns itself effort is foucs on farming agricultural aspect. So, this country has many farmers concentrate on farming agricultural aspect. May New Zealanders choose to spend time to produce different kinds of wines, e.g. wine or red grape wine is for the people are eating meat, or they are eating dinner.

When these New Zealanders their behaviors choose to do farming or agriculture to grow and produce different kinds of taste of white or red grape wine drinking products job. Themselves grape agriculture behavior will influence these New Zealanders themselves, they can learn how to improve different kinds of grape wine drinking products in order to achieve every kinds of white or read grape wines taste improving aim during their white or red grape producing process.

Why can New Zealander every individual white or read grape wine producers improve their white or read grape wine taste more easily? In behavioral economic view, it can explain that why any one New Zealander white or read grape wine producer can be encouraged or excited or persuaded to concentrate nervous and energy and effort to learn how to improve their white or red grape wine products easily.

In fact, New Zealand is one agricultural food export country. It has good natural environment resource , e.g. land, seed to provide any one farmer to produce themselves any kinds of agricultrual food products, e.g. fruit, or wine food products. Because New Zealanders know themselves country has enough natural resource . So, in common, many New Zealanders choose to attempt to do farming agricultural jobs in order to export themselves any kinds of fruit or meat or wine products to overseas or sell to domestic in order to earn profit.

So, when these New Zealand farmers number has been increasing every year. This country farmers will feel themsleves competition between this New Zealand farmers themselves are serious due to they may feel New Zealanders choose to do agriculture businesses in order to export themselves different kinds of farming food to overseas or sell to local to earn profit.

Hence, when many New Zealand farmers feel that farmers number has been increasing every year. They will feel themselves competition is serious. They must need to spend much time and nervous and effort to research what method is the best how to produce the best taste of white or red grape wine products in order to let local or overseas wine buyers to choose to buy his/her producing white or read grpae products to drink.

Hence, in competition psychological view, may influence many New Zealand white or reaad wine producers had been beginning to change their learning behavior on researching what method is the best in order to produce the best quality of taste red or white wine products to sell in order to attract overseas or local white or read grape wine drinkers to choose to buy his/her wine products. Their behavior will focus on learning how to raising or improving white or read grape wine taste method more than only focus on producing a large number white or red grape wine products. They believe wine quality is more important to compare wine producing number. So, New Zealand wine producers themselves wine producers behaviors have been changing on concentrating on researching wine quality method aspect more then wine producing number aspect in behavioral economic view.

America high technological productive behavior

For America example, US is one high technological country, it owns many high technological knowledge talent inventors, e.g. computer science inventors. Hence, US must attract many diferent countries owning high technological computer inventors choose to go to US to develop their computer science profession career. Also, it seems that when many computer science inventors or professions choose to go to US to develop themselves computer science new career. In behavioral economic view, due to their leaving themselves countries choice, which may bring influence themselve country job behaviors need to be changed. They must need to adapt US new live. Because they will forgive their past computer science job. These computer science professionals need to spend time to adapt US new lives. They " past computer science job behaviors" will need to be changed to their new US any computer employer's new computer science job model.

Because their traditional computer science jobs needed to be forgot in their themselves countries. They will feel their old computer science job knowledge and behavior needed to change in order to let their US any one new of computer company employer feels satisfactory to accept their new working behavior in any one US computer organization.

So, on the other hand, many US computer company employer will feel that they must need time to accept any one new overseas computer science professions their working behaviors, their working attitude daily, because these foreign comouter science professional, their past computer working behaviors and working attitude must be different to US domestic computer science professions.

In behavioral economic view, these overseas computer science professions, their working behaviors and attitude must be needed to change in order to adapt any one US new computer company itself domestic or local computer science professional stafs themselves daily working behaviors and attitude because these overseas and local computer science professionals must need to team work together.

In behavioral economic view, it is only one way that foreign computer science professionals must need to change themselves past country traditiona daily working behaviors and attitude in order to cooperate with these US local computer science professionals in teams more easily.

Consequently, if these foreign compute science professionals can change their past working behaviors and attitude to let any one US local computer science professional feels to cooperate with them easily in short time. Then, the US computer company itself whole computer professional teams themselves efficiencies will be influenced to raised or improved by the changing past working attitude and working behaviors of these foreign computer science professionals. So, in behavioral economic view, only if US any one computer company hopes itself computer teams themselves efficiency can be raised or improved when it decides to employ foreign computer science professionals and US domestic computer science professionals. They need to work in teams together. They must need to let these foreign computer science professionals to know how to change their working behaviors and attitude to let their domestic computer science professionals feel easy to work together. Then, the US computer company itself whole team efficiency must be rasied or improved easily in short time.

● China share market investing behavior

For China share market example, economic development depends on financial market. Because if many Chinese have interest to invest to carry on shares buying and selling activities in orde to learn how to earn shares interest and share profit when the China shareholder can make decision to sell himself/herself shares in the the high price, then he/she can earn money when he/she can sell the China company's shares in the high sale share price position.

If China has many Chinese like to spend time to carry on investing shares activities. Themselves shares buying and selling behaviors will influence China has many companies can increase fund from many Chinese shareholders in order to have enough money to expand or develop themselves businesses in China in long term. Consequently, when China can have many Chinese like to attempt to carry on buying and selling shares investing behaviors in China share market. Themselves buying and selling shares behaviors can help many Chinese companies have effort to increase enough money or capital in order to continue to do their businesses in long term absolutely. So, it explains why when many Chinese become shareholders , they can assist China will have many companies continue to develop their businesses if many Chinese like to carry on shares buying and selling investing behaviors in long time in China financial investment market nowadays in behavioral economic view.

Why has any individual country have many people invest share behavior which can influence the country's macro consumption desire?

I shall apply shares market buying and selling investment behavior to explaiin why shares investment behavior which may impact the country's overal consumption desire as below:

In behavioral economic view, I assume that when the coutry has many people have interest to attempt to carry on shares buying and selling investment behavior, then their frequent shares buying and selling behaviors which may bring negactive consumption desire or shopping desire of these shares investors their consumer behavior. The reason is simple, when the country has many share buyers number suddenly been increasing rapidly. Consequently, these large group share investors must need to spend much time to research any kinds of company shares variations, whether when their share prices will rise up of fall down in order to achieve buying the company's shares in the lowest price and selling the company's shares in the highest price level in order to earn profit.

Basic on this reason, they must need to spend much extra time to research share prices changing behavior every day, e.g. one working person will wait to leave his/her job, after he/she can spend time to gather data to research the day's share price changing behavior after dinner. So, the working person's right time may be his/her share price market research behavior. Before he/she may spend his/her night time to go to shopping after dinner, but nowadays, he/she will fogive to do his/her shopping behavior before dinner or after dinner at hight sometime. He/she will make decision to spend much night time to turn on computer to click on share market website to research his/her share purchase choice to investigate whether his/her share price whether it rises up or falls down at the moment in order to make his/her share buying or selling decision at ever night time.

I mean the when the country has many people are share investors, their shares investment behavioral spenging time which will influence many shops lose customers at might often because the country will have many people feel need to spend night time to turn on computer or watch television to investigate share price variation. So, the country will have many people / share investors choose to stay at home in order to carry on share price variation investigation behavior, they need to listen share market update news from radios or watch the share market update news from computer or TV at home every night. Consequenly, they must reduce times to leave themselves homes at night. So, their shopping behavior also will be reduced. Because these share investors feel need to spend time to investigate share price variation news at homes which can bring economic benefits (high opportunity benefits) when they choose to forgive to leave homes to go to shopping times (opportunity cost) every night.

On conclusion, it seems that when the country has many people are share investors, then their share price investigating behavior may bring negative shopping emotion at night. Consequently, the country's any one shop may lose many customers from this share investor consumer group in behavioral economic view. Hence, when the country's share investors number had been increasing rapidly, it will influence any shops lose many customers from this share investing customer group at night frequenly in short time, even long time in behavioral economic view, because their shopping desires or shopping emotion will be brought negative feeling when they make decisions to spend much time to listen radios or watch TV or computers share price update nes at night. Hence, share market will bring negative impact to influence consumer shopping desire or negative shopping emotion in behavioral economic view.

Can technology influence human shopping behavioral change?
Nowadays, technological development has reached mature stage, whether technological mature stage may bring positive or negative shopping emotion influence to global consumers. I shall aplly internet inventin or ecommerce shopping channel tool to explain whether internet technology can bring postive or negative influence to global consumer behavior in behavioral economic view.

Internet is a good technological tool, it brings e-commerce business chance. In fact, commonly, global has have many businessmen choose to use internet channel to carry on their products transactions between global online-buyers and their electronic websites. So, global many shoppers had begun to feel online shopping is more convenient to compare visiting shops shopping.

Their shopping behaviors have been changed from internet technological tool. Global has many shoppers choose to buy any products from any overseas or local businessmen their web stores. They only need to spend time to find any businessmen their webstores to choose the most suitable products to pay visa to buy from their webstores. at homes. So, in general, global had have may shoppers had changed their shopping behaviors from visiting shops to visiting webstores at homes often.

So, it seems that internet technological tool had influenced global many shops disappear, but internet webstores will be replaced their actual shops on streets. Some of businessmen either they choose webstores to replace shops or choose websotes and shops both or still keep shops only. Hence, internet tool influences global businessmen have three kinds of products sale channels to let globa local and overseas consumers to choose how to buy their products. However, in fact, many of global shoppers, youngers and olders had begun to accept to buy any products from webstores. They feel to spend time to leave homes to visit shops , their shopping behaviors will be wasted time to not essential part to their daily lives. Hence, since internet technological invention, it had changed many consumers their traditional visiting shops shopping habit to change to buying products from webstores channel.

However, on the one hand, internet creates webstores ecommerce shopping channel to let global many consumers do not need to leave homes to go to shopping. It brings negative visiting shops shopping emotion to global general consumers nowadays. But on the other hand, it also brings positive visiting internet webstores shopping emotion to global general consumer nowadays. So, it seems that global many consumers feel that they often do not need to spend much time to go out shopping. Many global consumers feel convenient and enjoy to choose any products to buy from different internet webstores, when the online buyer chooses the most suitable product, he she only needs to pay visa card to buy the product from the online seller's webstore conveniently at home.

Hence, online shopping can bring economic benefit to online

buyers, e.g. avoiding walking time or spending transport fare to visit the shop to go to shopping, shortening or reducing shopping time to do another important matter.

On conclusion, global many consumers began feel online shopping can bring more economic benefits on shortening shopping time, avoiding transport fare spending aspect. So, online shopping will be popular shopping behavior for future long time. It may encourage global many shoppers can make rapid shopping decision in short time in order to carry on any products buying transaction to global any one online shopper in short time easily in behavioral economic view. So, global many businessmen had begun to build themselves one attraction webstore in order to persuade different countries consumers to choose to click themselves webstores from internet channel to buy any kinds of products in short time easily.

So, internet technology had changed consumers traditional shopping behaviors to build positive online shopping emotion as well as raise online sellers' any products sale chance easily in behavioral economic view.

Why and how human behavior may influence the country's economic growth or recession?

When one country has many people choose to do the same matter for one period, whether their behavior may influence the country's pvera; economic growth or recession . I shall attempt to indicate cases toexplain their relationship as below:

For flowing rubblish behavioral case example, do you feel that when the country has many people often flow rubblish on the streets, instead of their flowing rubblish behavior may bring streets dirty? But, their flowing rubblish behavior may explain that this country has people may have enough money to buy food to ear, or enough cloths to wear, enough bottles of water to drink, even they may have enough money to buy new television, radio, refrigeraters , washing machines, desktops or laptops electronic home products from old to new to use in order to satisfy their living needs. So, when they flow old electronic home products, their flowing old home electronic products behaviors may seem that they have enough money to buy other new home electronic products to replace old home electronic products to use at homes.

However, it seems thaat this country ought have many people have jobs to do. So, many of them, they can easy to make purchase decison to flow any old home electronic products and buy any new home electronic products to use . Because this country has many people have jobs to do. So, they can often not use old home electonic products to become rubblishs to flow on streets after they had bought any kinds of new home electronic homes.

In fact, it also implies that this country's economy grows rapidly. So, many businesses can glow up rapdly. When they expanded their businesses, they must need to increase employees number in order to let they help themselves to raise productivity or serve their clients absolutely. So, when the country has many businesses can grow up, it seems that its economy must be better or it is improved to compare past. Due to many different kinds of home electronic products had been often bought to use by this country people in this period. So, this country's any streets can be observed that expensive electronic home products were flowed on streets anywhere. then, this country will have many electronic home products sellers can sell their home electronic products very easily. When this country has many people can find any kinds of jobs to do easily. So, due to unemploymen rate had been decreasing.

In behavioral economic view, as this many electronic home products rubblish country case, we can observe this country may have many people have jobs to do. So, consumption number has been increased long time. So, cheap food, or expensive home electronic products may be rubblish on any streets. This country's people , their flowing rubblish behaviors may be explained that many of people have enough jobs to do, so they have ability to buy any good taste food to eat or buy any kinds of expensive electronic home products to use. So, this country's economy may be improved for this long period. So, in behavioral economic view, when this country can have many electronic home products rubblishs are flowed on anywherer in streets frequently. It seems that this country will have many people have jobs to do, so it causes they often change old home electronic products or replaced them easily, when they have enough income to spend to buy any kinds of new home electronic products to use at homes easily. Moreover, their flowing old electronic home products behaviors also indicate that this country has many people their salaries may be increased in possible from their emplyers. When this country can have many different kinds of home electornic products are sold. It means that this country's electronic home products needs or demand had been increasing, due to many people have jobs to do and income increases to excite their living of needs also improve. Consequently, this country may seem have better economic improvement. We can observe from this country's electronic home products rubblish increasing income in theis period.

On conclusion, this country ought experience economic growth at this period. So, " flowing expensive electronic home rubblish increasing number " may seem that this country's economic growth is rapidly in this period, due to many people have jobs to do as well as salaries increase in this period.

Technology how impacts human behavior changing?

Technology how influences human behavior to bring changing? For example, online share purchase and sale transaction from smart phone brings share investor can do share buying or selling transation in any where and any time conveniently, non manual driving auto vehicle, bring car owner feels comfortable and spends free time to do other matter, e.g. reading, listening mucis in himself or herself car freely. electrical energy vehicle can help car owner to reduce air polluton and it can brings the drivers do not feel drive long time in any journeys in order to avoid air pollution for environmental protection responsible car drivers in our societies. Thus, they will drive long time in any journeys when they can drive electronic energy cars to replace oil energy cars.

However, online technology can also bring consumers can choose to stay at homes to buy any things from seller individual online webstore conveniently. Such as online technology can bring shoppers do not need to spend much time to visit shops to buy any things. They can choose any kinds of products from any online sellers individual online webstores conveniently at homes. Online technology excite busy consumers can make purchase decision easily as well as it can help online sellers sell any kinds of products from internet easily.

In behavioral economic view, technology can change human behavior to be improved, it can let human feels comfortable, more free time ro use, rapid making any decisions, such as apply smart phones to make share purchase or sale transaction decision, online shopping decision, even travelling any where decision in short time, when the traveller finds the most cheap hotel accommodation room price and air ticket price frm any travel agent online tourism webstore, then the potential travel customer can follow the online hotel accommodation price and air ticket price data to make decision when to buy the air ticket from the airline travel agent or make decision when to prebook which hotel accommodation room to go to the country to travel from online travel agent tourism webstores. So, technology can encourage global any country travelers to make anywhere to trvel rapidly. If the traveler can find the country's general hotel rooms and airline tickets prices had been decreasing more sightly. The traveler may make travel decision to choose the country to travel in short time, then he/ she can prebook the country;s any hotel room and airline ticket to pay by visa fraom the country's any hotel and airline travel agent webstores., before one week, even one month or more easily. Hence, online technology can also encourage traveler individual frequent travel times to be increased, due to global travelers can find any hotel rooms and airline tickets prices from internet conveniently at homes. They do not need to spend time to visit any airline travel agent to enquire travel choice country's hotel rooms prices and airline ticket prices. They can compare global travel of countries choices ' all hotels rooms and airline agents air tickets prices to make prebook airline seat and hotel room decision before one week, one month even six months early.

On conclusion, online technology can encourage global travelers can make travelling any where and when traveling time desicions easily. It can excite tourism industry develops in long time. Also, such as electricity cars invention can encourage environment protection car owners do car purchase decision easily, because they can choose to drive electronic energy cars to replace oil energy cars in order to avoid air pollution occurs easily. So, electronic cars can increase electronic car purchasrs number, due to many of environmental protection attitude of car owners can choose to drive electricity cars to bring air cleans, even non -manual driving cars can encourage lazy driving and free time driving car owners to choose to buy non-manual (artificial intelligent) cars to drive , because they can spend much free time to read, listen music or do any matters in themselves cars, they do not need to drive cars, robotic (AI) auto driving machine is such one non-manual driver to help them to drive themselves cars confidently. So, non-manual driving cars can attract lazy and enjoying free time driving car owners to choose to buy to replace traditional manual cars to drive easily. Moreover, online share transaction can help any share investors to make share buying and selling decision in short time easily. When they can apply smart phones technological tool to carry on share buying and selling activities easily. They can observe any share rising or falling price suitation from smart phones in any where any any time easily. So, smart phone technology can help global any shareholders to make share purchase and sale transaction easily. So, technology can encourage human makes decision in short time rapidly.

How and why employees behaviors may influence economy development?

In behavioral economy view,I believe the country's any organizational employees behavior may bring indirect relationship to influence the country's long term economic development. I shall indicate past manufacture industry social development period to explain their relationship. For many countries' past business activities had belonged to manufacturing industry, such as US, UK past before 1980 year, it focused on steel manufacturing and steel manufacturing related machine products. So, US, Uk developed countries manufacturing industries may be past main country's economic income sources. I assume US , UK past had one million number different kinds of industries. They ought had about seven houndred thousand number organizational businesses were belonged to manufactured industry. They may include:

Steel manufacturing and steel related machine manufacturing, e.g. vehicle manufacturing, home appliances, e.g. washing machine, television, radio, refrigerate cooler, heater, air condition etc. different kinds of different kinds of steel -related manufacturing machine, they were manufactured from US, UK steel machine manufacturers. So, US, Uk the other three hundred thousand number industry may be general service industry, e.g. hotel service, restaurent, cinema, public transport service, tourism lesiure , wine bar, supermarket etc. different kinds of non-manufacturing industries business organizations were operated in UK, US past before 1980 year.

So, in UK, US developed countries industry development history, they ought have high percentage of businesses belonged to steel related manufacturing machine and steel products. Also, in the past before 1980 year, US, Uk business employers , they employed many workers are manufacturing workers. They needed to spend long time to work in factories. They were skillful workers, and they are trained to manufacturing cars, washing machine, television, heater, etc. even steel itself different kinds of steel related products to prepare to deliver to their shops to sell to US, Uk local or overseas clients.

So, I believe that past UK, US ought employ many employees, they belonged to skillful manufacturing workers, manufacture increasing steel machine or steel related machine number of products rapidly daily. So, if UK, US had had many of these manufacturing factories owned high skillful workers, then their manufacturing steel-related machine or steel both kinds of products number must be influenced to raise rapidly. Consequently, their steel machine manufacturing products would been exported to overseas or would been sold to local both markets , they may be influenced to raise sale number. They (these manufacturing workers) needed to be trained to know how to manufactur these different kinds of machine products in the efficient teams and they ought to be trained to raise their efficiencies in order to shorten time to manufacturing many kinds of steel related manufacturing machine or steel itself products rapidly. So , if their efficiencies and manufacturing performance was improved, these US, UK any one manufacturing worker and their teams ought achieve raising productivities significantly.

Hence, when past UK, US manufacturing industry development period, if these two countries' any manufacturing factories could have many manufacturing workers could be trained to be skillful and proficient manufacturing workers. Then, in past every day to these factories workers, they ought help their steel or steel related manufacturing employers to raise any kinds of machine or steel products number in every team. So, when past in the manufacturing industry development, US, UK could have many factories' manufacturing workers themselves steel or steel related machine products manufacturing skill could be trained to to improve to any kinds of these machine or steel manufacuring products quality as well as their products number could be influenced to raise by themselves skillful improvement significantly every day.

Then, what would be influenced to occur to past UK, US manufacturing industry period? In behavioral economic view, when these two manufacturing industry developed countries, such as UK, US , if they had many factories workers can be trained to improve their skill in order to achieve any kinds of steel or steel-related machine products quality could be improved as well as products manufacturing number could be also increased absolutely. In consequence, past UK and US both countries ought increase themselves any kinds of steel and steel related machine products number to be supplied to themselves local shops to let local clients to choose any one kind of machine manufacturing products to buy easily as well as they could also export to supply overseas any countries to buy their different kinds of steel or steel related machine products to let overseas steel or steel related manufacturing machine product buyers, they can have many of these different kinds of these steel or steel-related different kinds of manufacturing machine from UK and UK these both countries easily to compare other countries.

On conclusion, I believe that past US, and UK macro manufacturing industry income GDP would increase significantly. So, they would have good economic growth performance because when many of these manufacturing workers themselves manufacturing effort could be improved. So, it explained when employees manufacturing abilities can influence economic growth indirectly.

Robots invention whether they can help organizations to raise efficiencies or inefficiencies?

In behavioral economic view, in any organizations, when the organization hopes its worker teams can raise efficiencies , the organization may choose to increase more workers number and/or it can provide training to improve these workets themselves skills in order to raise their efficiencies. For one warehouse example, when the warehouse increases many goods , they are needed to delivered these goods from the shelves to the delivering destination locations. If this warehouse supervisors feel these workers themselves goods delivery speeds are slow, which is possible due to this warehouse's workers number is not enough. So, this warehouse supervisor ought increase workers number in order to increase their goods delivery speed in order to deliver goods from the shelves to every indicated goods delivery destination in order to let any one lorry driver can transport the right kinds of goods and ensure the accurate goods number to transport to any one client home rapidly. However, if this warehouse supervisor planed to buy several warehouse goods delivery robots to assist these warehouse workers to find the right kinds of goods from shelves and then deliver to the right destination location in the warehouse. So, these warehouse orkers can concentrate on counting the accurate goods number and ensuring the right kinds of goods in order to prepare to let lorry drivers to transport these goods to these goods of buyers themselvers homes rapidly. Consequently, in the first step, robots can concentrate on finding th right goods from shelves and delivers them to the right goods transportation of location destination. Then, in the second step, these warehouse workers can concentrate on counting the accurate goods number and ensuring the right kinds of goods in order to prepare to put them to the lorry. Consequently, when warehouse robots and warehouse workers can cooperate to work together, the most important, robots, can deal on finding the right kinds of goods and deal on delivering the accurate number of goods of job duty as well as these warehouse workers can only concentrte on counting the right kinds of goods number in order to avoid it has none any mistake of wrong kinds of goods and inaccurate goods of delivery number to be transported to the lorry and to deliver to any one buyer's home.

So, it seems that warehouse robots ought help any one warehouse worker to raise himself efficiency and avoid goods delivery of mistake occurrence easily as well as their help to warehouse workers that can let any one goods buyer feels their goods can be delivered to their homes rapidly. Moreover, warehouse robots can also help these warehouse workers to raise efficiencies because warehouse robots can help them to shorten goods delivery time between any one shelf and any one goods delivery destination of location in the warehuse because robots may help them to find the right kinds of goods from the right shelf in the short time. So, any one worker does not need to spend long time to seek anywhere is the right shelf location for the kind of goods when the kind of goods are needed to deliver to the buyer's home from lorry. Warehouse robots can help them to do this aspect of " finding the goods from the right shelf in short time job duty". So, any one warehouse worker only needed tospend less time to do the counting of any right kind of goods number and ensuring the right kind of goods job duty. Consequently, this warehouse 's any one worker, his any one kind of goods delivery time may be reduced, because robots' assistance and they may have more confidence to avoid mistake to deliver the wrong number of goods and/or the wrong kind of goods to any one goods buyer's home.

On conclusion, it seems that warehouse robots ought may help any one warehouse worker to raise efficiency for any one team in the warehouse as well as the warehouse any one supervisor does not need to spend much time to observe any one worker individual performance for " goods delivery job duty aspect" because their goods delivery job duty that had been replaced to do by these several warehouse robots. Robots can achieve the more accurate of right kinds of goods and the right number of goods delviery job performance to compare any one of human warehouse worker themselves right kinds of goods of delivery and right number of goods of delivery job performance. So, when robots can participate to cooperate with this warehouse's any one worker to do their goods of delivery job duty in this warehouse every day. Then, robots can raies any one of supervisor individual confidence in order to let they do not need to spend time to observe any one of worker individual whose goods of delivery job performane. They can concentrate on supervising any one worker whose goods transport to lorry in the final step in order to avoid to deliver wrong goods number and / or wrong kind of goods to any one goods buyer's home every day. Consequently, this warehouse's overall teams of their delviery of goods performance many be improved by robotss' participatin to goods of delivery task as well as this warehouse's oveall teams themselves efficiencies may be influenced to raise by robots' goods of delivery task participation.

Why social behavior may influence organizational strategy needs to be changed ?

Why any organizations need to know whether nowadays social behaivor how has been changing in order to implement the kind of the most right strategy to achieve the profit aim pursue in possible. I shall indicate nowadays ecommerce or online, customer shopping behavior to explain above question concerns they ought have close relationship between social behavior and organizational strategic choice or organizational behavioral changing need.

On nowadays ecommerce business, or online shopping model, this kind of shopping model in global many young and old age consumers like to apply internet tool to choose any country sellers website stores in order to stay at home to buy any kinds of products from themselves webstores in global societies.

In fact, online shopping model had been popular for long time above to twenty years. Most of global sellers will make decision to design themselves webstores in order to attract global many online buyers to choose to buy their products from themselves webstores. So, it seems that social consumers purchase behaviors had been changed to online shopping from internet invention.

Hence, social consumers purchase behavioral changes may influence any organizations' strategies need to be changed from visiting shops purchase strategy model to online purchase strategy model, if the seller still concentrate on concentrate on considerate how to design itelf , but neglects to considerate how to design itself webstore, e.g. how to design attract product photos to put on itself webstore, how to arrange sale price information location to be putted on webstore and visa card payment location on itself webstore in order to let any one online buyer can feel very easier to buy itself any kinds of products from itself webstore. Then, its potential online buyers will be influenced to increase number when they can find this online seller itself any kinds of products photes and every kinds of product sale price information and visa card payment channel locations easily from itself webstore.

So, it implies that nowadays any one seller ought need to design one webstore to let any one online overseas and domestic consumers can have chance to click itself webstore to choose any one kind of product to buy conveniently when he/she does not hope to leave him/her home to go to shop, because nowadays social shopping behaviors had been influenced to change when internet invention, them it gives another online purchase method to replace visiting shops purchase method to global any one buyer in nowadays societies.

So, if nowadays any one seller still concentrate on how to design itself shop display in order to put any kinds of product on shelf in order to let any one visiting shop customer to find the kind of product to buy, but it neglects to change to choose to pursue another new technological shopping method, such as webstore purchase method in order to implement effective strategy to design the most right webstore as well as in order to attract global overseas and local consumers to find itself webstore easily from website and find its any one kind of product phots and sale price and visa card payment button in order to choose to buy itself any kinds of products in the short time. Consequently I believe that the seller will lose many customers from overseas and local when its other same or similar product sellers choose to design themselves webstores in order to let global any one product buyer can buy themselves any one kind of product when they can pay visa card to buy their products from them webstores conveniently when they stay at home habitly. Then, the seller will lose many global potential customers in long time.

On conclusion, in behavioral economic view, any consumer behavioral social changing, which will influence any in order to avoid customers number loses significantly . In future time, organizations need to make rapid decision in order to implement the most reasonable and the most useful strategy in order to avoid global potential customers number reduces or lose them in long time. So, social behavioral changing environment ought influence any global organizations need to decide how to change themselves strategies in order to avoid customers loses significantly in future time.

How and why human behavior may influence economic growth or recession?

May ourselves daily behaviors influence our global societial continue economic growth or recession? Do they have cause and effect close relationship between human behaviors and global economic growth or recession? I shall apply behavioral economic theory to analyze and explain whether ourselves daily behaviors and our global societial economic growth or recession which have close cause and effect relationship as below:

Every country itself economic development must depend on any business activities, otherwise, any kinds of business activities must need ourselves business activities or behaviors in order to achieve any business activities as well as achieve the country's overall economic development in macro view.

However, any country's overall business activites or behaviors which must depend on any kinds of individual businessmen, themselves employees daily working behavior or activity or performance in order to help them to attract or increase many clients number to acieve " earning profit" aim. So, it seems that any individual business, itself overall every department individual working behavior is one main factor to influence the company's overall business performance.

For agricultural fruit and meat food farming industry example, such as New Zealand is a farming main target industry country. It had had many New Zealanders were daily themselves own farming businesses for many years. Their farming businesses include growing fruit, sheep, cow, pig pork, meat etc. food sale business. If the New Zealand farmer owned a large size farming land, then he will choose either growing fruit or feeding sheeps, pigs, cows to be meat to to transport to New Zealand supermarkets to help them to sell to their farmers meet to New Zealanders in order to earn profit. Thus, if the New Zealand farmer owned large size of farming lands, then he needs to employ many farming employees (farming workers) to help him to carry on farming business daily tasks, e.g. picking up friuts, feeding pigs, cows, sheeps to eat food daily. These daily farming jobs are very important to influence this New Zealand farmer's meats or fruits sale number whether they can be easy or diffcult to sell in New Zealand supermarkets , if these farming workers can own encough farming knowledge or skill to know how to pick up fruits method and make judgement to know whether it is right time to pick up the kind of fruits from the trees , as well as know how feed this pigs, sheeps, cows to eat food in order to let they are better health. Consequently, their farming behaviors which can let these animals can provide the best taste and enough meat from these animals to let New Zealander to buy to eat from New Zealand any one supermarket. Even these New Zealand farming workers can know whether the kinds of fruits, e.g. oranges, apples, gapes etc. fruits whether they ought be picked up from the trees at the right time. Consequently, they can make judgement to decide to pick up any kinds of the best taste fruits to let any one New Zealander to buy to eat from any one supermarket in New Zealand. Otherwise, if they do not make judegement to know whether the kind of fruit ought not be picked up because they still need longer time to continue grow up to increase fruit size and better taste from the trees in order to let any one fruit buyer can feel better taste when they eat this kind of fruit later. If they can buy this kind of fruit to eat later, then this New Zealand farmer's his fruit buyers can buy the best taste of this kind of fruit to eat from an yone supermarket in New Zealand. Consequently, many New Zealand supermarkets will choose to buy any kinds of fruits from this farmer fruit supplier when they feel this farmer's fruits can provide more better taste fruits to compare other farmers' fruits.

Thus, due to New Zealand is one farming main income source country. It's any kinds of fruits and meats need to be export to overseas to sell , instead of local sale. It's GDP percent is very high to whole country 's overall income source. So, any one New Zealand farmer individual and any one farming worker individual working behavior will influence its economy whether it is influenced to grow or recession possible. Moreover, it also seems that farming workers' farming knowledge and skill will influence themselves farming daily activities to achieve the aim of the number of increase or decrease to any kinds of fruits whether they are better taste or the number of increase of decrease to any kinds of meats whether they are better taste to supply to any one New Zealand fruit or meat buyers to eat from any one New Zealand supermarket. So, it implies that any one New Zealand farming worker individual farming behavior may influence any kinds of fruits or any kinds of meat taste because they are transported to any one supermarket to sell in New Zealand.

Consequently, if New Zealans had many farmers can teach god farming knowledge and skill to let their any one farming workers know how to decide judgement to decide when it is right time to pick up any kinds of fruits from trees , or how to grow them on soil in order to let they can grow rapidly. Then, many different kinds of fruits can be provided to let any one New Zealanders can eat the best taste of fruits when their fruits are supplied to any one New Zealand supermarkets. Even, if they knew how to feed foods to pigs, cows, sheeps to eat daily. Then they can be more health and they can provide the best taste of meats to let any one New Zealanders can buy their meats from any one New Zealand supermarkets. Moreover, their fruits and meats can be transported to overseas to let any one country fruits or meats buyers can choose any kinds of New Zealand meats and fruits to buy to eat from themselves countries supermarkets. Then, many overseas fruit and meat buyers will perfer to choose New Zealand any kinds of fruits or meats to buy to compare other countries fruits or meats to buy when they go to any one local supermarkets.

On conclusion, it seems that New Zealand farming workers themselves farming behavior may influence their farming employers any kinds of fruits or meats sale number and income because their farming task behaviors must influence whether their fruits or meats taste are the better taste or worse taste to compare their other local farmers (the farmer competitors) whose fruits or meats taste. If tthe farmer's any one farming worker can be trained to learn how to know to feed animals skill and when is the most right time to pick up any kinds of fruits from trees or how to grow them on the soil methods. Due to these farming worker individual farming behavior may influence his different finds of fruits and meats sale number to be increase or decrease, so these any one

New Zealand farmer must need to depend on any one farming worker whose farming working methods, if their farming working behaviors can be the best to influence any kinds of fruits to grow rapid or any kinds of pigs, cows, sheeps animals grow up rapidly , then their sale number may be increase significantly and their taste can be improved to let any New Zealand or overseas meat or fruit buyer to buy to eat to feel from any one New Zealand or overseas supermarkets, then New Zealand's agriculture industry must be influenced to increase. In the world, any one fruit or meat buyer must choose to buy New Zealand's fruit and meat to eat in prefer to compare other countries' fruits and meats. So, New Zealand's GDP may be influenced to raise from any one New Zealand farming worker individual farming working behaviors.

www.ingramcontent.com/pod-product-compliance
Lightning Source LLC
Chambersburg PA
CBHW020624160726
47991CB00002BA/921